The Coming World Revival

Other Books by Robert E. Coleman

Established by the Word
Introducing the Prayer Cell
Life in the Living Word
The Master Plan of Evangelism
The Spirit and the Word
Dry Bones Can Live Again
One Divine Moment (Editor)
Written in Blood
Evangelism in Perspective
They Meet the Master
The Mind of the Master
Songs of Heaven
Growing in the Word
The New Covenant
The Heartbeat of Evangelism
Evangelism on the Cutting Edge (Editor)
The Master Plan of Discipleship
The Spark That Ignites
Nothing to Do but to Save Souls
The Great Commission Lifestyle

The Coming
World Revival

*Your Part in God's Plan
to Reach the World*

Robert E. Coleman

CROSSWAY BOOKS • WHEATON, ILLINOIS
A DIVISION OF GOOD NEWS PUBLISHERS

To Alathea, Angela, and Jim,
my precious children and
members of the household of God—
with enduring love

In the last days, God says, I will pour out my Spirit on all people. Your sons and daughters will prophesy, your young men will see visions, your old men will dream dreams. Even on my servants, both men and women, I will pour out my Spirit in those days, and they will prophesy. I will show wonders in the heaven above and signs on the earth below, blood and fire and billows of smoke. The sun will be turned to darkness and the moon to blood before the coming of the great and glorious day of the Lord. And everyone who calls on the name of the Lord will be saved.

ACTS 2:17–21 NIV

Contents

Foreword

T HE GREATEST NEED AMONG CHRISTIANS AND churches today is for genuine spiritual revival—revival that comes not from man but from God Himself. Whenever God has touched His people in special times of revival, lives have been changed, and Christians have experienced new power to do God's work. Truly revival is the spark that ignites.

Drawing upon his thorough understanding of both the Bible and church history, Robert Coleman points the way to true revival. A revived condition, he rightly states, should be the normal situation of God's people. But all too often sin makes us complacent, dulling our spiritual sensitivity and blocking the channel of God's blessing. Only when we face our need of repentance and seek God's forgiveness and power will we experience the full measure of new life He has for us.

Revival also means we begin seeing the world the way God sees it as we reach out to others with the Gospel and with deeds of loving service.

No one is better qualified than Robert Coleman to write on revival, both by training and by experience. No one in our generation has a clearer vision of God's plan for His people or a greater burden for revival.

So I am thankful that Dr. Coleman has written this volume. It is one of those rare books that speaks both simply and profoundly, challenging each of us to a deeper commitment and a greater openness to what God wants to do in us and through us. It could be one of the most important books you will ever read.

More than twenty-five hundred years ago the prophet Habakkuk cried, "O Lord, revive thy work in the midst of the years." May that be our cry also.

BILLY GRAHAM

Introduction

Something Is Missing

GOD'S PEOPLE EVERYWHERE INCREASINGLY YEARN FOR something more in the life of the church. We go through the motions of religion, but there is no power. For many the thrill of personal devotion is gone. The joy of the Lord has leaked out; there is no spring in our step, no shout in our soul. A spiritless boredom is the norm.

All the while the world plunges deeper into sin. Aimless multitudes, having no sense of their true nature created in the image of God, debase human dignity in public and private. The sacredness of home and family is forgotten. A spirit of lawlessness hangs like a heavy fog over the land.

But the day of reckoning is sure to come. Moral and spiritual decline has its limits. The time comes when we must reap the folly of our ways. Already we are beginning to see the disintegration of our foundational social institutions. Unless something happens to change our course, civilization as we know it cannot endure.

It's Easy to Despair

Little wonder that many people despair. It is easy to become pessimistic when problems seem overwhelming.

I recall an amusing story of a woman who became so distraught that she responded negatively to everything. One day she was venting her frustrations on her family as they were riding in the car when suddenly a dog darted across the road, and her husband slammed on the brakes. The abrupt stop jerked the wife upright while their child went tumbling to the floor. Turning to her husband, the exasperated woman cried, "Oh, Arnett, you've killed him!"

About that time the little boy came crawling out from under the seat. "Mama," he whimpered, "I'm not dead."

"Hush up," she retorted. "Yes, you are!"

Unfortunately, I am afraid that is the way we may unconsciously react to the discomforting situation in our world. Everything looks so dark that a better future seems impossible. For some, this feeling may be intensified with the sense that we are living in the end time of our age.

But That Means There's Hope!

We need to remember that it is usually in periods of momentous crisis that great revivals are born. Our sense of helplessness, properly directed, actually can make us more sensitive to the need for supernatural grace. It is not until the night closes in that we look up and see the stars.

The last days preceding our Lord's return are no exception. In the twenty-fourth chapter of Matthew where we are promised that the Gospel will be preached in all the world before the end comes, Jesus also told how the period will be marked by mounting tribulation. Perilous times seem to go hand in hand with the fulfillment of the Great Commission. I do not know if we belong to that last generation, but whatever the divine schedule, we are living in a day of tremendous spiritual opportunity. Indeed, we could be the very people who will see the long-awaited outpouring of the Spirit across the earth before the coming of the great and glorious day of the Lord.

Even now amid the gathering shadows some encouraging signs appear. The growing burden for prayer among God's people around the world, the rising awareness in our churches of the believer's discipleship lifestyle and ministry, the multiplication of little groups in homes and schools meeting for Bible study, the increasing number of youth catching the vision for global missions, the surge of evangelism and church growth in many areas of the world formerly closed to the Gospel—these and many other contemporary movements in the body of Christ portend great things for the future.

Notwithstanding the superficiality of so much going on in our religious activity, a growing host of people are seeking something deeper. They may not be theologians, but they know God is alive, and they long to know Him in a living relationship. Ceremonial rites and pious clichés, however orthodox, have not satisfied their souls. Nor has the glitter of big buildings, big budgets, and big programs answered the cry of their hearts for spiritual reality.

Call it what you may, these honest men and women are searching for revival—a God-wrought transformation in the inner being that reaches into the total fabric of life and culture. Here is the challenge before us. Unless we face it coura-geously, we are irrelevant to the needs of our day.

Why This Book?

Some twenty years ago I wrote a manual on revival (I will use the terms "revival," "renewal," and "awakening" inter-changeably) entitled *Dry Bones Can Live Again*. That book has since gone through many printings with a number of translations into other languages. Later it was enlarged and published under the title *The Spark That Ignites*. What I tried to say in those pages is more pertinent today than it was then, and much of it is said again in this present volume. However, I have revised the material while updating it, giv-ing more attention to the hope of a coming mighty world revival.

With the Church moving toward that future day, my emphasis centers upon principles of spiritual awakening now—considerations basic to any authentic ministry. The pri-mary focus is on the meaning of revival in our own lives—what it does, how it comes, when it may be expected—and to relate this to practical ways we can have a part in God's plan to disciple all nations.

The book is designed to help you examine the issues from the Bible. It can be used as an introductory text on revival; or in a more specific way, it may be used as a prepa-ration manual for special revival services in the church. In either case, it is intended as a source book for personal and group study.

In recognition of the many demands upon your time, only the most crucial matters relating to revival are presented, and the treatment is deliberately brief. An attempt is made to facilitate further research by documenting references and noting other resource books and articles. In this regard a serious student will find the footnotes very helpful.

The value of this study on revival lies in the extent to which you permit yourself to become involved with the subject. Try to complete the assignments. Make the personal applications. And as you do, sincerely pray, "Lord, send a revival, and let it begin with me!"

One

"Revive Us Again"

T HE PSALMIST PRAYED, "WILT THOU NOT REVIVE US again: that thy people may rejoice in thee?" (Psalm 85:6). He recognized that the people of God were spiritually impotent; the fires of devotion were burning low; their joy was gone. "Revive us," he cried, but what did he mean? What is revival?

Many today think of revival as a series of meetings designed to whip up interest in the church. Others think of it as some kind of religious emotionalism. Yet I doubt that these popular associations of the term ever entered the mind of the psalmist.

Revival: Restoring Life's True Purpose

Revival means to wake up and live. The Old Testament word for revival comes from a word meaning "to live," which originally conveyed the idea of breathing, inasmuch as breath is the expression of life in all animate beings. Hence, it could be said of the dry bones: "I will cause breath to enter into you, and ye shall live" (Ezekiel 37:5; cf. 37:6, 14; Job 33:4; 1 Kings 17:22). Revival, or life, was "breathing in the breath of God." As used here, the idea emphasized is that the source of this life is in God.[1]

The comparable New Testament word means "to live again" (Revelation 20:5; Romans 14:9; cf. 7:9). As Jesus used the term, it denotes the change in the life of a penitent prodigal who returns to the father's house, in the sense that the son who was "dead" is now "alive again" (Luke 15:24, 32). Other words liken revival to the rekindling of a slowly dying fire (2 Timothy 1:6) or to a plant that has put forth fresh shoots and "flourished again" (Philippians 4:10).[2]

The basic idea of revival is always the return of something to its true nature and purpose. In terms of redemptive history, revival can be seen as that "strange and sovereign work of God in which He visits His own people, restoring, reanimating and releasing them into the fullness of His blessing."[3] By its power, "vast energies, hitherto slumbering, are awakened, and new forces—for long preparing under the surface—burst into being."[4] In the wake of revival comes life—life in its fullness, life overflowing with the love and power of God.

Not everything about this new life can be fully explained, of course. Since it is a supernatural work of the Spirit, there is always the element of mystery about it.[5] But one thing is clear—in revival men and women come alive to the life of God.

Personal Transformation

Revival becomes evident by the change wrought in the heart by the Holy Spirit. The extent of its penetration will vary, and there will be differences in its mode of expression, but revival is manifest "wherever you see (spiritual life) rising from a state of comparative depression to a tone of increased vigor and strength."[6]

The most immediate transformation is in the renewal of individual Christian experience. When one responds fully to divine grace, there is a wonderful assurance of sins forgiven; the heart is clean; the soul is free. Faith does not stagger at the promises of God. Prayer pulsates with the fragrance of heaven. Love fills the heart with singing, and there is spontaneous praise. There is still suffering and temptation, but amid it all is the light of God's face shining in the inner man. Christ is real; His peace sweeps over the soul; His victory overcomes the world.

From the standpoint of New Testament Christianity there is nothing unusual about the revival experience. It is the way a person should always live. In the words of Roy Hession: "It is just you and I walking along the highway in complete oneness with the Lord Jesus and with one another, with cups continually cleansed and overflowing with the life and love of God."[7]

Or as Charles G. Finney explains, revival simply "consists in obeying God,"[8] which means that it is the most elemental duty of man.

Revival in this personal sense should be a constant reality. The idea that revival is a "thing of special times and seasons"[9] comes from the inconsistent nature of man, not from the will of God. Unfortunately, most of us experience those times of spiritual sluggishness that make revival necessary. But if we lived in the continual fullness of the Spirit of Christ, as God desires, revival would be an abiding state.[10]

New Vitality for the Church

Yet revival involves more than personal blessing. As individuals come alive to the reality of Christ and this experience is multiplied in the lives of others, the church feels a new unity of faith and purpose—a genuine fellowship in the Spirit.[11] For when believers are brought near to the living Head of the body, they are "brought nigh to each other in holy love."[12] This does not imply lock-step agreement on every issue, but to a remarkable degree revival creates an environment whereby sincere disciples of truth come together and minor differences are resolved in the larger commitment to a common mission.[13]

The love of Christ filling our hearts moves us to care for those whom God loves and for whom He gave His Son. Out of this compassion the dynamic for a compelling evangelism is born. The commission to make disciples of all nations cannot be ignored. In the same spirit, social concern is quickened for oppressed and afflicted people.[14] Duty becomes a joy. Love naturally overflows when hearts are full.

Society inevitably feels the impact of renewal among Christians. As the Gospel goes forth in word and deed, the world takes note that men and women have been with Jesus. Sinners are moved to seek the Savior. Restitutions are made. Broken homes are reunited. Public moral standards improve. Integrity makes its way into government. To the extent that the spirit of revival prevails, mercy, justice, and righteousness sweep over the land.[15]

Human Hindrances

Of course, human factors can hinder revival—materialism, for example. Or cultural prejudice that refuses to yield to the new spirit of love. For that matter, any perversion of righteousness will hinder revival. And because society is infiltrated completely by human depravity, revival will always have an uphill battle.

Opposition will be most pronounced from those who do not want a spiritual dimension of life. Some will be repelled by the personal moral changes called for by the revival; others will resent its social implications. Whenever practical holiness is manifest, antagonism can be expected from the carnal mind that is against God. Such antagonism may even come from within the religious community.[16]

We should remember, too, that there are human failings even among those who experience revival. Regrettable as it is, spiritual renewal does not make one any less a finite man or woman. Ignorance, emotional instability, personality quirks, and all the other traits of our fallen humanity are still very much in evidence. Though the revival is not responsible for these shortcomings, it has to bear their reproach.[17]

The Divine Hallmark

Nevertheless, wherever the spirit of revival is felt, attention focuses not on human weakness but on divine power. It reveals One who makes the earth His footstool and who sees nations as dust on the scales of His judgment. In the might of His holy arm, "human personalities are overshadowed and human programs abandoned." Man retires "into the background because God has taken the field."[18] In stripping away the artificiality of human achievements, revival creates a situation where the grace of God is magnified. Christ is lifted up, and honest hearts bow in adoration before Him.

Overshadowing it all is the awe-inspiring reality of "the presence of the Lord" (Acts 3:19). This is the witness of revival that has no counterfeit—the overwhelming sense of the Holy Spirit drawing men and women to Christ and making them an instrument of blessing to others. Where this is in evidence, the world has to admit that God is alive.

Some Accounts of Revival

Jonathan Edwards, renowned pastor at Northampton, Massachusetts, might be cited as one witness to the reality and power of revival. Describing the effect of a great outpouring of the Spirit in his parish in 1735, he said:

> As the number of true saints multiplied . . . the town seemed to be full of the presence of God: it never was so full of love, nor of joy, and yet so full of distress, as it was then. There were remarkable tokens of God's presence in almost every house. It was a time of joy in families on account of salvation being brought unto them. . . . On whatever occasions persons met together, Christ was heard of and seen in the midst of them. . . . The Spirit of God began to be so wonderfully poured out in a general way through the town, people had soon done with their old quarrels, backbitings, and intermeddling with other men's matters. The tavern was soon left empty. Every day seemed in many respects like a Sabbath day.[19]

Edwards noted, too, that "there were many instances of persons who came from abroad on visits" to the town, who "partook of that shower of divine blessing," and as these visitors "went home rejoicing," soon "the same work began to prevail in several other towns in the country."[20]

The Korean revival early in this century is another example of what happens when the Spirit of God takes over. A missionary who attended a church meeting during the flood tide of this outpouring said:

> The room was full of God's presence . . . a feeling of God's nearness impossible to describe. . . . The whole audience began to pray. . . . It was not many, but one, born of one Spirit, lifted to one Father above. . . . God came to us in Pyeng Yang that night. . . . Man after man would arise, confess his sin, break down and weep. . . . My last glimpse of the audience is photographed indelibly in my brain. Some threw themselves full length on the floor; hundreds stood with arms outstretched towards heaven. Every man forgot each other. Each was face to face with God.[21]

As is true in every genuine revival, the overflow of God's Spirit did not cease with the blessing of the people gathered for prayer at Pyeng Yang. The account goes on to say that when the men returned to their homes in the country, they took the Pentecostal fire with them.

> Everywhere the story was told the same Spirit flowed forth and spread. Practically every church . . . throughout the peninsula received its share of blessings. . . . All through the city men were going from house to house, confessing to individuals they had injured, returning stolen property and money, not only to Christians, but to non-Christians as well. The whole city was stirred.[22]

The events leading to the consecration of the new cathedral in Coventry, England, in 1962, furnish an example of a more contemporary renewal experience. Stephen Verney, an Anglican priest, tells how a group of laity and clergy got together to seek the Lord. As they allowed love, humility, and prayer to flow through them, "a deep sense of the presence of God" filled their lives.

Out of this fellowship came the idea for a deeper-life mission that eventually involved the whole diocese. As Verney describes it:

> The more deeply people were involved, the more clearly was God calling them to go deeper still and to offer him the obedience of their whole lives. . . . The diocese became a person, a body alive with a spirit. . . . We experienced an extraordinary outburst of worship and happiness. . . . Great services were held in the new cathedral, offering up to God every part of our daily lives. . . . We have seen reality break through like the sun through a fog, sweeping away the pretenses. People have been set free to become what they really are. We have begun to know that a whole diocese could be a fellowship of the Holy Spirit.[23]

There it is again. That same sense of the divine presence thrilling the church with reality of life and mission.

A Personal Witness

To these accounts I might add a vivid experience of revival in my own life. It was in 1970 during the turmoil caused by the Vietnam War. While students on many campuses were rioting and burning down buildings, students at Asbury

College in Wilmore, Kentucky, were strangely drawn to their knees one morning to pray. Classes were forgotten. Academic work came to a standstill. In a way awesome to describe, God had taken over the school. Caught up in the wonder of it, a thousand students remained for eight days and nights in the college auditorium—not to demand more freedom, but to confess their sin and to praise their Lord.[24]

"I've never seen anything like it," one veteran newscaster told his television audience. Then he asked his viewers to put down their newspapers, stop whatever they were doing, and watch the revival scene he had filmed earlier in the day. "Though I've seen it," he concluded, "I still can't believe it."

It began on February 3 during the regular chapel service. The speaker that morning finished early, so he invited students to use the time to testify. After one or two had spoken, a senior rose and confessed that during his years at college he had been a phony. As the tears streamed down his face, he told of the emptiness of his Christian profession and asked his classmates to forgive him for his hypocrisy.

No sooner had the man sat down than a young lady stood and shared a similar burden. Everyone sensed that the Spirit of God was very near. Students began coming forward to pray. They filled the altar, overflowing into the aisles and front seats. Earnest supplications erupted through tears of repentance. The bell rang announcing the end of the period, but no one left to go to class. There was more important business at hand. Nothing mattered now but getting right with God.

A student captured something of the feeling that day as he jotted impressions in his diary:

I sit in the middle of a contemporary Pentecost. A few
moments ago there came a spontaneous movement of the
Holy Spirit. . . . The scene is unbelievable. . . . Witness is
abundant. Release—Freedom—Tears—Joy unspeakable—
Embracing—Spontaneous applause when a soul celebrates.
A thousand hearts lifted in songs of praise and adoration
to a mighty God.[25]

For eight days and nights it lasted—185 consecutive hours
without interruption. Even when classes finally resumed,
every evening after supper students would gather in the auditorium to pray and celebrate what God was still doing. The
lights in the building were not turned out for four months—
until after commencement in June. Before the initial effect of
the revival had subsided, practically every person in the college and seminary had felt the touch of heaven, and the witness was carried by Spirit-filled students and faculty to
hundreds of other schools and churches across the land.
Fires of faith were lighted that have since spread around the
world—and still are burning in many hearts.

Wonderful Variety

What happened at Asbury could be duplicated in some way
every time there is revival. Yet the particular manner in
which it comes will change. The spirit of the time, local circumstances, personal leadership, temperament of the people,
and many other natural conditions combine to give each
revival its own distinctive color. Likewise the methods
employed in revival may vary in different times and among
different people.[26]

While basic spiritual principles are common to all revivals, these principles emerge in human situations in such different ways that it is impossible to predict their precise form. God seems to delight in surprising His people with the unexpected freshness of His approach.

We can be grateful for this variety in God's providence, for it demonstrates that He is ever seeking to make His will more intelligible to His people. Yet it also serves to remind us that God is able, when He pleases, to confound the schemes of men. Human manipulation cannot put the Spirit in a straitjacket. What He does in revival is by His own sovereign power, and no man dare take any credit for the work.

Revival's Key Role in Church History

No matter how revivals come, they are the high peaks in the Christian life. Whether in individual experience or in the corporate life of the church, it is during these times of refreshing that the work of the Holy Spirit is brought into bold relief.[27] Redemptive history could actually be written from the standpoint of these recurring revivals.[28] Of course, in the sense that revival represents vital Christianity, it can be said that a deep revival undercurrent is always present, in varying degrees, in the spiritual life of the church. But in revival seasons this stream breaks forth in great power, affecting many people and sometimes changing the course of nations.

This can be seen frequently in the Old Testament, but it comes to its fruition at Pentecost with the emergence of the New Testament Church. For three centuries the spirit of revival continued to dominate the persecuted and impoverished Christian community. However, as the church gained in worldly prestige, eventually being recognized as the state religion of Rome in the fourth century, spiritual fervor noticeably declined.

Though somewhat smothered by the ecclesiastical policies of the Church, revival fires still burned in the hearts of a faithful remnant. And from time to time this smoldering flame would burst forth. There were seasons of refreshing under such leaders as Augustine in the fifth century, Justinian and Gregory in the sixth century, and John of Damascus in the eighth century. During the dark Middle Ages (roughly A.D. 1000 to 1500) the cause of revival remained alive in such movements as those of Bernard of Clairvaux, Francis of Assisi, Peter Waldo, John Towle, John Wycliffe, and Savonarola.

The Protestant Reformation had many ingredients of a revival, calling the Church back to God and the Bible. The Anabaptists especially deserve recognition for their fervent spirit of evangelism that blazed a trail of heartfelt faith across Europe. When the Church became dominated by scholastic disputation, the Pietist, Puritan, and later the Wesleyan revivals breathed new life upon the dead bones. From these revivals, missionaries scattered out over the world, and in many areas the churches they established have experienced great outpourings of the Spirit.

Our American Heritage

To a remarkable degree, revivals have molded the course of the church in America.[29] Peter G. Mode of the University of Chicago says that "more than any other phenomenon, they have supplied the landmarks of our religious history."[30]

William Warren Sweet has characterized these revivals as "cascades in the stream of the church, recreating the main course of its waters."[31] Were it not for these seasons of refreshing during several crucial periods when the very existence of the republic was in jeopardy, it is doubtful that our country could have survived.

Unfortunately, in recent years the experience of revival has declined. Many true disciples of Christ have kept the reality alive, and from time to time scattered local areas have seen general outpourings of the Spirit. Nevertheless, no real national awakening has come in our lifetime.[32] We cannot expect to drift much longer.[33]

"Lord, Do It Again"

Years ago, after the funeral of General William Booth of the Salvation Army, the sexton found a lone Methodist preacher on his knees at the altar. Thinking of the tremendous impact of the life of this one man upon the world, the preacher was praying, "O Lord, do it again! Lord, do it again!"

As you think about the great times of revival in the past and then consider the desperate situation today, do you not find yourself also praying that God will do it again—that men and women will come forth who believe God for the impossible and that their numbers will increase until a new and mighty demonstration of holy love sweeps across the land? God grant that it may be so! "Wilt thou not revive us again: that thy people may rejoice in thee?"

Study Assignments 1

Personal Study

The following questions are intended to help you get a biblical perspective on the lesson and make some personal applications. You may want to take a question or two during your private devotions each day. Normally a lesson can be completed in a week, although you may want to extend the time on some of the later lessons. Try using a small notebook to record your answers.

1. Meditate upon Psalms 80:18; 85:6; 138:7. What does revival mean in these passages?

2. Where is the source of this spiritual life? Note Isaiah 57:15 and Deuteronomy 6:24; 32:39.

3. What is the blessing of revival described in Hosea 6:1-3 and 14:7?

4. A great revival occurred during the reign of King Hezekiah. Read the account of this period in 2 Chronicles 29:1–32:31. List some of the blessings that accompanied this revival, noting the biblical references.

5. As you interpret revival in terms of your own situation, can you see some areas where your experience of victorious Christianity could be enlarged? Note three.

6. How do you feel your church can experience revival?

7. What would be the effect of real revival in your community?

8. Write out in your own words the prayer of Habakkuk 3:2. Preserve the spirit of the prayer, and yet phrase it in terms appropriate to your own situation.

Group Discussion

After completing the personal study, discuss your ideas with people who share your concern about revival. You may get together at stated times outside the regular church schedule, or if this is not convenient, meet during the regular service of your prayer meeting, Sunday school, or evening worship. Six to eight people make a good group, though you may have a few more. Whether you meet as couples or individuals does not matter, but it is wise to keep generally within the same age level.

One person can be designated leader of the group. If you desire, this leadership can be rotated. The leader is responsible for keeping the discussion alive and drawing out the participation of each member. A good procedure is to ask questions that call for a definite personal opinion, such as, "John, what does this mean to you?" When questions arise, the leader may refer them to another person, for example, "Jim, how would you answer John's question?"

The groups should plan to meet for an hour or so, depending upon the circumstances. Usually the first part of the period is given to sharing insights gained in personal study. The latter part should be a time of prayer, remembering especially needs that have been expressed during the meeting. And don't forget to praise God.

For this first meeting, let each one read his or her definition of revival from question one. Then some can give their answers to questions two through four. If you care to mention it in the group setting, answers to questions five through seven can be read. After this, let each person tell his or her most memorable experience of revival in the church. Be perfectly free in expressing your views. To conclude, some can read the prayers they recorded in question eight.

NOTES

1. Altogether this word is used in its various forms more than 250 times in the Old Testament, of which about 55 are in the *Piel* or causative construction in Hebrew. Some examples may be found in Genesis 7:3; 19:32, 34; Deuteronomy 6:24; 32:39; 1 Kings 20:31; 2 Kings 7:4; Nehemiah 4:2; Job 36:6; Psalms 41:2; 71:20; 80:18; 119:25, 37, 40, 50, 88, 93, 107, 147, 154, 156, 159; 138:7; 143:11; Jeremiah 49:11; Ezekiel 13:18; Hosea 6:3; 14:7; Habakkuk 3:2, to cite a few. It may be translated as revive, live, restore, preserve, heal, prosper, flourish, save, or some other similar term.

2. A word for revival is used only seven times in the Greek New Testament, although the idea is suggested in other ways. Perhaps one reason for the sparing use of this term, as compared to the Old Testament, is that the New Testament narrative covers only a generation, during which time the Church for the most part enjoyed a remarkable degree of spiritual life.

3. Stephen F. Olford, *Heart Cry for Revival* (Westwood, N.J.: Fleming H. Revell, 1962), 17. This little book of expository sermons on revival is solidly biblical and warmly written. It is excellent reading on this subject. A comparable book is A. Skevington Wood's *And With Fire* (Fort Washington, Pa.: Christian Literature Crusade, 1958).

4. James Burns, *Revivals, Their Laws and Leaders* (Grand Rapids: Baker, 1960), 39. First published in 1909, this book is a classic in its field. Its treatment of laws observable in revivals is unsurpassed for beauty and simplicity of expression. Andrew W. Blackwood has written two summary chapters in this reprint edition.

5. In *Revival, an Enquiry* (London: SMC Press, 1954), 14, Max Warren correctly observes that true revival is continuous and changing, and therefore

"any finality of assessment would be premature." With a development so "alive" as this, the "attempt to pigeon-hole it is futile, for the pigeon will not stay in the hole."

6. William B. Sprague, *Lectures on Revival of Religion* (London: The Banner of Trust, 1959), 7, 8.

7. Roy Hession, *The Calvary Road* (London: Christian Literature Crusade, n.d.), 31.

8. Charles G. Finney, *Revivals of Religion* (Westwood, N.J.: Fleming H. Revell, n.d.), 1. This volume consisting of twenty-two lectures has remained in print for more than a hundred years and is probably the most influential text on the subject.

9. Arthur Wallis, *The Day of Thy Power* (London: Christian Literature Crusade), 19. The author in this excellent book prefers to think of revival in terms of great mass movements that stand out in history. As to what usually is given recognition, his point may be well taken, but I see no need to limit revival to these spectacular and occasional displays of God's sovereign power.

10. An excellent treatment of this idea is Norman P. Grubb's little book, *Continuous Revival* (Fort Washington, Pa.: Christian Literature Crusade, n.d.). The author mentions how he was shaken out "of the misconception of years, that revival could only come in great soul-shaking outpourings of the Spirit." Of course, he rejoices in the times when the church was mightily stirred in "precious hurricanes of the Spirit," but as he says:

> I saw the defeatism and almost hopelessness that so many of us had fallen into by thinking that we could do nothing except pray, often rather unbelievingly, and wait until the heavens rent and God came down. But now I see "revival" in its truest sense in an everyday affair right down within the reach of everyday folk to be experienced in our hearts, homes and churches, and in our fields of service. When it does break forth in greater and more public ways, thank God; but meanwhile we can see to it that we are being ourselves constantly revived persons, which of course also means that others are getting revived in our own circles (6).

11. Warren, *Revival*, 19-37, distinguishes between revival as a church-directed movement and enthusiasm as a more individualistic experience. He observes that personal enthusiasm outside the structure of the church usually results in magnifying personal blessings to the detriment of the larger body of believers. Very likely this observation oversimplifies the situation, but it at least points up a real danger in revival movements.

12. John Bonar, *The Revival of Religion* (Edinburgh: The Banner of Truth, 1984), 8. This book is a compendium of addresses by Scottish evangelical leaders delivered in Glasgow in 1840.

13. Genuine revival is the key to any ecumenical movement, since it brings out the dynamics of true Christian unity. Church history demonstrates this. If popular spokesmen of the drive for church union were as much concerned for spiritual revival as for organizational structure, there would be more progress in true Christian unity.

14. Revival is a catalyst of social reformation. It produces the kind of concern and environment for things to happen that can radically change human behavior and institutions. Merely to try to improve human conditions by social action alone does not solve the basic problem in society. This is the fallacy of the so-called modern social gospel, which does not come to grips with the basic problem of sin in the human heart. Until something is done to regenerate the sinful nature of man, any social program is superficial.

On the other hand, the Gospel has a clear social application, and until this is realized, we have not understood its relevance to our whole life. Genuine revival fuses the personal and social aspects of the Gospel. Again a study of Church history will bear out this conclusion. Contrary to the impression given by liberal theologians, many great humanitarian movements have had their roots in evangelical revivals. For example, revivals gave impetus to the movement for the abolition of slavery, the organization of trade unions, abolition of child labor, women's suffrage, the start of hundreds of benevolent and missionary societies, the founding of our first colleges and the YMCA, to name just a few.

The modern "social gospel" itself actually grew out of the midnineteenth-century revivals, although in time the humanitarian concern has tended to lose much of its evangelical content. A well-documented study of this thesis is Timothy Smith's *Revivalism and Social Reform* (New York: Abingdon Press, 1957). J. Edwin Orr's Ph.D. dissertation at Oxford, published as *The Second Evangelical Awakening in Britain* (London: Marshall, Morgan and Scott, 1949), also brings out the tremendous social effect of these nineteenth-century revivals, as does his more recent study, *The Light of the Nations* (Grand Rapids: Wm. B. Eerdmans, 1965). A less extensive approach to the subject is Frank G. Beardsley's *Religious Progress Through Religious Revival* (New York: American Tract Society, 1943). See also the thoughtful treatment of social concern in the context of revival by Richard F. Lovelace, *Dynamics of Spiritual Life* (Downers Grove, Ill.: InterVarsity Press, 1979), especially pages 355-400.

15. William G. McLoughlin, *Revivals, Awakenings, and Reform: An Essay on Religion and Social Change in America, 1607-1977* (Chicago: University of Chicago Press, 1978), xiii. McLoughlin describes these larger movements as "awakenings," or periods of "cultural revitalization" usually extending over a generation or so, as distinguished from "revival," which has its reference more in personal experience. However, the two terms are commonly used interchangeably, as I do in this study.

16. Revival has a way of making people face issues to such a degree that neutrality becomes difficult. Consequently, those who refuse to measure up may become overly critical of the movement and even seek to counteract its influence. The building friction may eventually result in schism. Incidentally, such schisms during times of revival led to the founding of many of our Protestant denominations and colleges.

17. Because revival does release the soul from bondage, it is not surprising that excessive demonstrations of spiritual freedom sometimes occur. In this sense, as Max Warren observes, "revival is a perilous experience." But, he wisely concludes, "the perils must be set beside the perils of Laodicea. More often than

not there is the choice." Warren, *Revival*, 21. For further insight on the place of emotion and ecstatic experience in revival, see John White, *When the Spirit Cometh with Power* (Downers Grove, Ill.: InterVarsity Press, 1988).

18. Wallis, *Power*, 20. For a beautiful statement of this truth, see the address of James I. Packer, *God in Our Midst: Seeking and Receiving Ongoing Revival* (1987), available in book or video format from Pastoral Renewal, P. O. Box 8617, Ann Arbor, Mich. 48107.

19. Jonathan Edwards, *A Faithful Narrative of the Surprising Work of God in the Conversion of Many Hundred Souls in Northampton and the Neighboring Towns and Villages*, in *Puritan Sage, Collected Writings of Jonathan Edwards*, ed. Vergilius Ferm (New York: Library Publishers, 1958), 169, 170, 177.

20. Ibid., 171.

21. Told by Dr. William N. Blair in his book *Gold in Korea*, and quoted by Kyang Check Hon in his address included in *One Race, One Gospel, One Task*, vol. 1 (Minneapolis: World Wide Publications, 1967), 109-11. Used by permission.

22. Ibid., p. 112.

23. Stephen Verney, *Fire in Coventry* (Westwood, N.J.: Fleming H. Revell, 1964), 24, 26, 35, 36, 51.

24. The story of this revival is told by eyewitnesses in *One Divine Moment*, ed. Robert E. Coleman (Old Tappan, N.J.: Fleming H. Revell, 1970). In many ways the movement was similar to the Asbury revival in 1950, some accounts of which I cited in my book *Dry Bones Can Live Again* (Old Tappan, N.J.: Fleming H. Revell, 1969), 20-23. First-hand reports of the earlier awakening are recorded by Henry C. James, *Halls Aflame* (Wilmore, Ky.: Department of Evangelism, Asbury Theological Seminary, 1966). For a broad summary of college awakenings over the past two and a half centuries, see the well-documented study of J. Edwin Orr, *Campus Aflame* (Glendale, Cal.: Regal Books, 1971).

25. Jeff Blake, quoted in Coleman, *Moment*, 27.

26. A running summary of the way methods are adapted to changing cultures and conditions may be found in the book by Paulus Scharpff, *History of Evangelism* (Grand Rapids: Wm. B. Eerdmans, 1966). This study of the historical and theological roots of modern evangelism covers Germany, England, and America for the past three hundred years.

27. As noted above, spiritual vitality seldom follows an even course. Human nature being what it is, there seem to be periods of lifelessness, times when there is only a halting response to the Spirit's appeals; then after a period of lethargy, an awakening may come. James Burns notes that the Psalms are a good example of this variation in spiritual sensitivity. At one time the writer, caught up by an inflowing wave of blessing,

> . . . exults in his strength, his heart rejoices in God, though a host should encamp against him, he shall not be afraid. But this jubilant note does not last; soon, caught in the trough of the wave, his voice cries out for help, his heart is in despair, light and hope alike seem to have forsaken him. From this he is rescued by the hand of the Lord and carried forward in a new tide of joyful, spiritual experience.

Burns observes that this fluctuation in experience actually serves to call our attention to the work of God. In fact, he believes Christians would tend to take God's life for granted were it not for these cycles of depression and exaltation. Burns, *Revivals*, 26, 27.

28. Much yet needs to be done in this field, especially in terms of world Church history. What is presently available is generally limited to particular times or areas. A book that gives a brief yet broad sweep of history is Milton L. Rudnick, *Speaking the Gospel Through the Ages: A History of Evangelism* (St. Louis: Concordia Publishing House, 1984).

29. The history of American revivals has been variously treated by many historians. A few of the more general works are F. G. Beardsley, *A History of American Revivals* (New York: American Tract Society, 1904); W. L. Muncy, *A History of Evangelism in the United States* (Kansas City: Central Seminary Press, 1945); Fred Hoffman, *Revival Times in America* (Boston: W. A. Welde, 1956); Bernard A. Weisberger, *They Gathered at the River* (Boston: Little, Brown, 1958); and a more biographical approach, Keith J. Hardman, *The Spiritual Awakeners* (Chicago: Moody Press, 1983). For an excellent bibliography on revival from the Great Awakening to the present, especially focused on the American scene, see Earle E. Cairns, *An Endless Line of Splendor* (Wheaton, Ill.: Tyndale House, 1986), 345-65. Further bibliographic information on revival may be found in Gerald Ina Gingrich, *Protestant Revival Yesterday and Today* (New York: Exposition Press, 1959); Nelson R. Burr, *A Critical Bibliography of Religion in America*, 2 vols. (Princeton: Princeton University Press, 1961); and Richard O. Roberts, *Revival* (Wheaton, Ill.: Tyndale House, 1982).

30. Peter G. Mode, *The Frontier Spirit in American Christianity* (New York: Macmillan, 1923), 41.

31. William Warren Sweet, *Revivalism in America* (New York: Charles Scribner's Sons, 1944), xv.

32. I am aware that some historians see spiritual awakenings recurring throughout this century, and I see no point in making this an issue. For every manifestation of spiritual renewal, including the large increase in church membership, we can rejoice. However, as I have defined revival, I hold to the opinion here regrettably expressed.

33. A realistic yet hopeful perspective on what to expect is Lewis A. Drummond's *The Awakening That Must Come* (Nashville: Broadman Press, 1978). With keen historical insight Drummond finds encouragement in some present renewal movements, while recognizing the necessity and conditions for deeper revival in the future.

Two

The Conditions for Spiritual Renewal

SINCE REVIVAL IS THE WORK OF GOD, WE MIGHT ASK why it is delayed. Surely the compassions of the Lord fail not. In the light of our great need, why doesn't revival come?

God Sets Conditions

Some cast the responsibility for spiritual renewal completely upon God. As humans we can do nothing about it—we must simply wait upon the Lord. This view correctly emphasizes the absolute sovereignty of God. But when God's sovereignty is made an excuse for indifference, then sovereignty is misunderstood.

Certainly revivals are God-sent. As a display of sovereign grace, they are entirely supernatural. Yet God does not violate His own integrity in sending them. Revivals must be consistent with God's Word.

Where God's conditions are met, we can be confident that revival will come. As Charles G. Finney put it: "Revival is the right use of the appropriate means. The means which God has enjoined . . . produce revival. Otherwise God would not have enjoined them."[1] Hence, "if we need to be revived, it is our duty to be revived. If it is our duty, it is possible."[2] Billy Graham stresses the same principle when he says, "I believe that we can have revival any time we meet God's conditions. I believe that God is true to His Word and that He will rain righteousness upon us if we meet His conditions."[3]

This conclusion is only logical since God always wants the best for his people. When the spirit of revival does not prevail, it is purely a human failure to exercise God-given privileges of grace. Never can a thrice-holy God be held responsible for the degenerate condition of the world or the Church.

It is not a question then of God's ability or desire to send revival. The question is: Do we want God's will to be done? If we dare say yes, then we commit ourselves to remove any impediment in our lives that would hinder revival. Furthermore, we obligate ourselves to do it now. God's will is clear. The next move is up to us.

Submitting to God's Word

Underlying this whole concern, of course, is the recognition of divine authority. There is no point in talking about revival unless we believe that God means business. "If my people, who are called by my name, will humble themselves and pray and seek my face and turn from their wicked ways, then will I hear from heaven and will forgive their sin and will heal their land" (2 Chronicles 7:14 NIV).

Again He promises, "If . . . you seek the Lord your God, you will find him if you look for him with all your heart and with all your soul" (Deuteronomy 4:29 NIV).

When we are willing to line up with God's Word, there is no limit to His blessing. "'Test me in this,' says the Lord Almighty, 'and see if I will not throw open the floodgates of heaven and pour out so much blessing that you will not have room enough for it'" (Malachi 3:10 NIV). "The Lord will give grace and glory: no good thing will he withhold from them that walk uprightly" (Psalm 84:11).

A thousand other promises declare the same provision. God is always for us. If we who are evil know how to give good things to our children, how much more will our Father in heaven "give the Holy Spirit to them that ask him" (Luke 11:13). Why then should anyone struggle on in spiritual defeat when all the resources of grace are available to the obedient heart?

But do we really believe what God says? This question must be voiced at the beginning, for everything else depends on our response. Obviously, if there is some doubt about the trustworthiness of God's revealed Word, there is likely to be little concern to measure our life by it. Systems of thought that discredit the holy Scriptures never produce revival.

Let us be clear at this point. The Bible is not incidental to revival.[4] As the eternal Word of God, it is the objective authority for all that we believe and practice. Apart from its immutable truth, standards of justice and holiness would degenerate into little more than whims of public opinion.

Even our knowledge of Christ, the living Word of God, would be lost in confusion and uncertainty if it were not for the unwavering testimony of Scripture. The Bible, and the Bible alone, is our basis for determining what to believe. It is the instrument of all divine blessing, the means through which the Holy Spirit ministers to our yearning hearts the grace of God.

Submission to the Bible's authority is the first require-ment for revival. God has sent forth His Word. To Him every knee should bow (Isaiah 45:23). When God speaks, we must listen. It is not our place to change or minimize the message. Nor are we called to defend what God says. The Bible is not on trial; we are. Our place is only to trust and obey. Once this is settled, our hearts are open for spiritual instruction.

Confessing Sin

The Word gives us an authority for our faith, but it also makes us face ourselves before the refining eyes of God's holiness. We see ourselves in the light of Jesus Christ. In His sight our righteousness is as filthy rags (Isaiah 64:6). The props of self-sufficiency are knocked out from under our pride. We are found out for what we are—sinners.

As the dreadful sense of guilt increases, the awful real-ization of impending judgment deepens. A holy fear grips our hearts, and we may be left with the feeling of utter helpless-ness. There is no place to hide from God.

One thing is certain—when the Spirit truly convicts our souls, however it may be felt, sin cannot be treated with indif-ference. Frivolity and lightheartedness are gone. We do not have to be urged to flee from the wrath to come. When we are broken and contrite in spirit, our hearts are disposed to heed any offer of mercy. In times of complacency it may be necessary to beg men to come to Christ, but in the throes of revival "sinners beg Christ to receive them."[5]

Once we have been awakened to our need, we must do something about it. Conviction of sin leads to repentance. There can be no revival until we confess our sin, turn from our evil ways, and throw ourselves upon God's mercy. "If I regard iniquity in my heart, the Lord will not hear me" (Psalm 66:18).

Any impediment to the flow of God's grace must be removed—unbelief, lust, lying, cheating, unclean thoughts, filthy speech, dirty habits, cursing, ingratitude, indifference to responsibility, disregard of self-discipline, prayerlessness, robbing God of tithes, Sabbath-breaking, neglect of the poor, racial discrimination, an unforgiving spirit, backbiting, envy, jealousy, bitterness, deceitfulness, selfishness, hypocrisy. Whatever it is, whether a deed or a disposition, if known to be contrary to the holiness of God, it must be confessed and forsaken.[6]

There can be no compromise. Repentance is a thorough housecleaning. Not only must confession be made to God; we must do all we can to make things right with people we have wronged. If we try to trim the corners and excuse a few favorite shortcomings, we are fooling ourselves. No revival can come in our hearts until sin is out of the way. Furthermore, until this is true of our own lives, we stand in the way of God's blessing to others.

The great New Hebrides Islands revival of 1949 is a splendid example of the role of repentance in revival. Led by their minister, a little group of earnest Christians entered into a covenant with God that they would "give Him no rest until he had made Jerusalem a praise in the earth" (Isaiah 62:7, author's paraphrase). Months passed, but nothing happened. Then one night a young man arose from his knees and read from Psalm 24: "Who may ascend into the hill of the Lord? And who may stand in his holy place? He who has clean hands and a pure heart. . . . He shall receive a blessing from the Lord. . . ." (vv. 3-5 NIV).

The young man closed his Bible and, looking at his companions on their knees, said, "Brethren, it is just so much humbug to be waiting thus night after night, month after month, if we ourselves are not right with God. I must ask myself, 'Is my heart pure? Are my hands clean?'"[7]

As the men faced this question, they fell on their faces in confession and consecration. That night revival came to the town. The whole community was shaken by the power of God, and within a few weeks the revival had moved across the island sweeping thousands of people into the kingdom.

So every revival begins. God can use a small vessel, but He will not use a dirty one. An Achan in the camp will always have an influence for evil upon many others. Let us be sure that our hearts are clean. "Search me, O God, and know my heart: try me, and know my thoughts: And see if there be any wicked way in me. . . ." (Psalm 139:23-24).

Prevailing in Prayer

When the channel is clean, the Spirit of God can flow through the believing heart in true intercessory prayer.[8] Such prayer is wrought from hearts overwhelmed with the sense of unworthiness yet captivated by the knowledge of God's forgiving grace.

When the revival was sweeping through Wales in 1904, a man who visited one of the meetings stood up and said, "Friends, I have journeyed into Wales with the hope that I may glean the secret of the Welsh revival." Instantly, Evan Roberts, leader of the revival, was on his feet, and with an uplifted arm toward the speaker, he replied, "My brother, there is no secret: Ask and ye shall receive!"[9]

That's it! Revival comes when God's people prevail in prayer.[10] "As soon as Zion travailed, she brought forth her children" (Isaiah 66:8). Jesus has promised, "I will do whatever you ask in my name. . . . You may ask me for anything in my name, and I will do it" (John 14:13-14 NIV; cf. 15:7, 16; 16:23-26). The name of Jesus, of course, is just another way of expressing the person and work of the Master. To pray in His name is to pray in His character, to pray in His Spirit, to pray as Jesus Himself is praying as mediator before the Father.

Prayer implies our complete identification with the purpose of God. Jesus called out in the inner depth of human emptiness, "Not my will, but yours be done" (Luke 22:42 NIV; cf. Matthew 26:39; Mark 14:36). His prayer was not passive submission to the Father, but a determined plea that God's will prevail over all else. Prayer has its joys, and it always throbs with thanksgiving, but supremely it is seen in Jesus to be active conformity to the will of God.

Where this condition is fulfilled, nothing is impossible (1 John 5:14-15). Whatever limits are imposed upon the power of prayer are entirely of our own making. We can go through all the forms of prayer, but until we actually want

God's will to be done and His glory to be revealed in Christ, we are not in the spirit of prayer.

Such praying is never easy. It will make us face the Cross. It will mean deep searching of soul and real sacrifice. When Jesus prayed in Gethsemane, the burden of His mission was so great upon His heart that while He prayed, "his sweat was as it were great drops of blood falling down to the ground" (Luke 22:44). Prayer was indeed the sweat, blood, and tears of His ministry (Hebrews 5:7). Everything else was easy in comparison to His intercession before the throne of God. The battle of Calvary was fought and won in prayer.

So it is with every victory of grace. The weapons of this warfare are not fleshly but are "mighty through God to the pulling down of strongholds" (2 Corinthians 10:4). As Sidlow Baxter has put it, "men may spurn our appeals, reject our message, oppose our arguments, despise our persons— but they are helpless against our prayers."[11] Satan has already defeated us if we try any substitute. Believing, persistent, determined prayer is the only way of victory. We can do more than pray after we have prayed, the godly A. J. Gordon has reminded us, "but we cannot do more than pray until we have prayed."[12]

Prayer Prevailed in Charlotte!

A little group of praying Christian businessmen in Charlotte, North Carolina, illustrate this principle so well. During the depression of 1932 they became greatly concerned about the spiritual and moral decay in their city.[13] Believing that the situation called for an all-out evangelistic effort, they asked the ministerial association to undertake a united crusade, assuring the clergy of their support. However, the ministers, somewhat skeptical of this type of meeting, declined the request.

Though disappointed, the laymen still felt that God wanted to do something big in their city. At a loss to know what else to do, they decided to call for a day of prayer. All who could were asked to come to a quiet, wooded spot on the outskirts of Charlotte and spend the day waiting upon the Lord. Twenty-nine persons responded to that first invitation. As they fasted and prayed, the faith of the men grew stronger. They prayed that God would be pleased to send a revival to their city and that it would spread over the state and out to the ends of the earth. This time proved such a blessing that in the months following, similar meetings were called. Two of these were held on the farm of W. Frank Graham, a dairyman and devout churchman who shared the men's concern for revival. Particularly was he burdened for one of his own children, William, a teenage boy who needed to come to grips with God.

Out of these repeated times of prayer the men felt led to sponsor an evangelistic meeting in the city. In the summer of 1933 they purchased a small tent and set it up for gospel services. This effort was so encouraging that the men decided to undertake a much larger crusade the following year. The Reverend Mordecai Ham was invited to preach. They encountered many difficulties in getting ready for the meeting, and several times it seemed as if the crusade would never materialize, but the men persisted in their prayers and labors. Finally in the fall of 1934 the Charlotte Crusade began.

What happened in that meeting is now well known. For

it was there that the young boy Billy Graham, along with many others, was converted. A spark was ignited in his life that has blazed a trail for God around the world.

Yet when I see the tremendous ministry of this great evangelist and thrill at the way God has used him to challenge so many with the claims of Christ, I cannot help but think of that little group of earnest Christian laymen, along with Billy's dad, down on their knees in the piney woods of North Carolina imploring God to show His omnipotence in a new way.

That is the way revival begins. It always starts in prayer as we seek first the kingdom and commit our lives for God to use as He pleases. When we truly take sides with heaven and pray with Christ, inevitably there will be fruit (John 15:1-17).

Reaching the Lost

One thing more needs to be stressed. Prayer leads to action. We cannot expect God to pour out His blessing unless we are willing to become involved in some kind of redemptive service. Yielding our lives to the Spirit's control means that we must make ourselves available for God to use in answering our prayers.

Whatever form our service might take, at its heart will be world evangelism—bringing all nations by all means to know Christ. If we are not occupied by this concern, we are a contradiction to the spirit of our loving Lord who came "to seek and to save that which was lost" (Luke 19:10). It is silly to talk about going all the way with Christ when we are neglecting the work to which He gave His life.

An atheist once wrote in derision:

Did I firmly believe, as millions say they do, that the knowledge and practice of religion in this life influences destiny in another . . . I should esteem one soul gained for heaven worth a life of suffering. Earthly consequences should never stay my hand nor seal my lips. Earth, its joys and its grief, would occupy no moment of my thoughts. I would strive to look upon eternity alone and on the immortal souls around me, soon to be everlastingly happy or everlastingly miserable. I would go forth to the world and preach it in season and out of season, and my text would be "what shall it profit a man if he gain the whole world and lose his soul?"[14]

A young, wealthy, carefree cricket player in England read these words, and though he tried to dismiss them, he could not escape their challenge to his indifference. Finally sheer honesty brought C. T. Studd to his knees, and he made a full commitment to Christ. Giving up his fortune, he became a missionary spreading seeds of revival across two continents. When people wondered why he did not spare himself in his passion to get the Gospel to those who had not heard, he replied, "If Jesus be God and died for me, then no sacrifice can be too great for me to make for Him."[15]

Isn't this really what it means to bear the cross of Christ (Mark 8:34; Matthew 10:38; 16:24)? The cross is not a physical infirmity, nor is it some difficult problem of our environment, as some people suppose. The cross is where Jesus freely gave His life for our redemption. Its purpose centered in saving a lost humanity. When we embrace the cross as our

way of life, do we then not commit ourselves to the purpose
for which Christ bore the cross for us?

Here finally is where we must face the issue. It is well
enough for us in the Church to sing about the cross on which
the Prince of Glory died, but what is more to the point is for
us to come down into the affairs of this world and take up
that cross ourselves. We must offer our bodies in living dedication to His ministry of reconciliation. Without this giving
of ourselves to reach those Christ loved and died to save, our
spiritual experience is not likely to mean much to the world
or to the Church.[16]

Jesus prayed that this sense of mission would captivate
the allegiance of His disciples. Just as He had dedicated
Himself "for their sakes," so also He prayed that they might
be sanctified by the Spirit (John 17:18-19).[17] Through their
witness, and in turn through the witness of those they won,
the world would come to believe in Him (John 17:20-21).
The fruitfulness of His ministry, indeed, the fulfillment of
His whole incarnate life, death, and resurrection depended
upon their faithfulness to this commission. Had they
remained self-centered and unwilling to accept the challenge,
the world would never have known the Gospel, and we
would be lost without hope today.

Would that we could see this dimension of holiness in
our lives! Many of us spend so much energy cultivating our
piety that we make it a substitute for active outreach to the
world. We get so wrapped up in our worship exercises,
deeper-life conventions, and sometimes even our revivals
that we have no time or energy for soul-winning. Certainly
we must feed our souls by Bible study and spiritual medita-

tion, but spiritual indigestion will likely occur if this devotion does not find an outlet in practical service.

I am reminded of Charles Spurgeon's comment in a church meeting after reading the verse, "And there came a messenger unto Job, and said, The oxen were plowing, and the asses feeding beside them":

> "Yes," [Spurgeon] said, lifting his eyes with a kindly glance around the crowded gallery, "that is still the case. Some of us are always plowing, breaking up the fallow ground, preparing the ground for good seed. And others are feeding. I know some of you dear people. You would not miss a service if you could help it. Feeding, everlasting feeding. It is good to feed, it is necessary to feed, but do a bit of Gospel plowing as well, for the health of your souls and the glory of God. The oxen were plowing, but the asses were feeding!"[18]

The Issue Must Be Faced

The disciples spent nearly three years feeding as they traveled with Jesus. There were times when they did some plowing, as when their Lord sent them out two by two to minister, but for the most part they seemed content just to enjoy their fellowship with Jesus. If they were ever to be much use to the kingdom, they needed to become involved much deeper in the work of Christ. Merely having their names written in the Book of Life was not enough to bring hope to others. They needed to come to grips with the real heartbreak of a lost world. Every deep-seated ambition and secret pride at cross purposes with God's program had to be crucified. In that utter emptiness of complete consecration they had to tarry until the reality of Christ's presence filled their lives. Then they could go forth in power as witnesses to the world. There was no use trying to get by on less. God promised them the fullness of His Spirit, and there could be no real revival without it.

Even so it is with us today. We, too, must look to the source of our life and, through the mighty power of the Holy Spirit, experience what it means to love God with all of our hearts, minds, and strength and to love our neighbors as ourselves. Nothing else will suffice.

Make no mistake about it! The responsibility for revival rests with us. Moreover, the conditions are clear. We must lay hold upon the surety of God's Word. We must confess our sin and turn from our deceitful ways. We must pray in the faith that God answers according to His will. And putting our lives at His disposal, we must work to bring men and women to Christ. Each of these conditions is merely a different way of saying the same thing: Christ must be exalted on earth as He is in heaven. When this happens, there is revival.

Study Assignments 2

Personal Study

1. Conditions for revival are listed in 2 Chronicles 7:14. After thinking through this verse, write it out in your own words, using contemporary language.

2. Condense to a sentence the condition for revival as proclaimed in Joshua 24:14-15.

3. Read the account of revival in 1 Samuel 7:1-17. What was the secret of this season of refreshing? Note especially verse 3.

4. Read the record of revival under Asa in 2 Chronicles 14:1-15:19. How would you sum up the condition for God's continuing blessing according to 15:2?

5. Read the account of revival under the leadership of Josiah in 2 Chronicles 34:1-35:27. Why was Josiah qualified to be a leader of his people? What brought the king and the nation to face up to God's expectations?

6. Study the lesson on fruit-bearing in John 15:1-17. What is the fundamental condition for bringing forth fruit (vv. 4 and 5)? How does the life of Christ enter you (vv. 3, 7, 10)? What privilege does fruitfulness (abiding in Christ) give you (vv. 7, 16)? What is the supreme demonstration of Christ living in you (vv. 9, 10, 12-14, 17)? Spiritually speaking, what do you think pruning means; and why does God prune the branches on His vine (v. 2)?

7. Why did Jesus link His sanctification with His mission to a lost world (John 17:18-20)?

8. What does bearing the cross mean to you? Is there something you can do to make your cross more real? Specifically what?

Group Discussion

Following the same plan as before, designate someone to lead the group. Be sure that everyone is acquainted. To start the discussion, one or two people can read their paraphrases of 2 Chronicles 7:14. Then move to question two, letting someone read a summary statement. This procedure can be followed on through the other questions, allowing for discussion as there is need. If time starts to get away from you, go on to the last question where the personal application is made. Each person might be asked to sum up what is felt to be the greatest need in his or her life. These personal concerns, along with the general burdens of the church, can be made a subject of prayer in closing.

NOTES

1. Charles G. Finney, *Revivals of Religion* (Westwood, N.J.: Fleming H. Revell, n.d.), 5. Many have taken exception to Finney's view of revival because he said that it was not a miracle in the sense that the laws of nature were suspended. However, Finney did not mean that revivals were naturalistic in the sense that people brought them to pass. In his reaction to extreme Calvinism, Finney was merely trying to emphasize the imperative of human responsibility in using the means provided by God. "But means," he said, "will not produce a revival, we all know, without the blessing of God. It is impossible for us to say that there is not as direct an influence or agency from God to produce a crop of grain as there

is to produce a revival. . . . A revival is as naturally a result of the use of the appropriate means as a crop is of the use of its appropriate means." For more information on Finney and his views on revival, see Lewis A. Drummond, *The Life and Ministry of Charles Finney* (Minneapolis: Bethany House, 1985).

2. Ibid., 33-34.

3. Billy Graham, "We Need Revival," in *Revival in Our Time* (Wheaton, Ill.: Van Kampen Press, 1950), 76-77.

4. A discussion of this principle in the history of the Church is A. M. Chirgwin's *The Bible in World Evangelism* (New York: Friendship Press, 1954); cf. Arthur Johnston, *World Evangelism and the Word of God* (Minneapolis: Bethany Fellowship, 1974). A recent illustration of the Bible's place in awakenings is the Indonesian revival, one of the great spiritual movements of our time. Already more than a million people have been brought to Christ through the witness of this revival, and the work is still going on. For one account of how it started with a little boy who brought home a New Testament and began to read it to his family, see the article by Stanley Mooneyham, "Indonesia: From Slumber to Revival," *Decision* 8, no. 12 (December 1967): 3, 13.

5. C. E. Autrey, *Revivals of the Old Testament* (Grand Rapids: Zondervan, 1960), 21. A moving description of conviction in revival may be found in Oswald J. Smith's *The Revival We Need* (London: Marshall Morgan and Scott, 1940), 45-56.

6. For a searching inventory of sins common among Christians, read Horatius Bonar's *Words to Winners of Souls* (Minneapolis: World Wide Publications, reprint, 1994). I can scarcely read this little book without falling on my knees.

7. Reported by Duncan Campbell, leader of this revival, as quoted in Arthur Wallis, *The Day of Thy Power* (London: Christian Literature Crusade), 124.

8. The cleansing that we receive through the blood of Christ enables us to assume the role of a priest before God, and our ministry in this capacity finds its highest expression in prayer for others. Hence the whole purpose of redemption while we live on this earth culminates in intercession. In *True Evangelism* (London: Marshall, Morgan and Scott, 1919), Lewis Sperry Chafer made a forceful and concise statement on this subject:

> The personal element in true soul-winning work is more a work of pleading for souls than a service of pleading with souls. It is talking with God about men from a clean heart and in the power of the Spirit, rather than talking to men about God (93).

This idea is also developed in S. D. Gordon's *Quiet Talks on Prayer* (New York: Grosset & Dunlap, 1941), 7-70.

9. Quoted from an unpublished account of the Welsh revival in Wallis, *Power*, 112.

10. An excellent treatment of this subject may be found in Finney, *Revivals*, 49-114. His lectures on "Prevailing Prayer," "The Prayer of Faith," and "The Spirit of Prayer" reflect the passion of one who believed that God always grants the request of a true prayer of faith. Among the more contemporary appeals for such praying are the stirring books by Leonard Ravenhill, *Revival God's Way* (Minneapolis: Bethany House, 1983); Sammy Tippit, *Fire in Your Heart* (Chicago:

Moody Press, 1987); Paul E. Billheimer, *Destined for the Throne* (Minneapolis: Bethany House, 1983); Wesley L. Duewel, *Touch the World Through Prayer* (Grand Rapids: Zondervan, 1986); and Joe Aldrich, *Prayer Summits* (Portland: Multnomah Press, 1992).

11. Sidlow Baxter, quoted by Cameron V. Thompson, *Master Secrets of Prayer* (Guatemala: Service of Life Schools), 4.

12. Gordon, *Quiet Talks*, 18.

13. An account of this laymen's group is given by Edward E. Ham in *The Story of an All-day Prayer Meeting and the Revival When Billy Graham Found Christ* (Wheaton, Ill.: Sword of the Lord Publishers, 1955). It is also alluded to in the biography by John Pollock, *Billy Graham* (New York: McGraw-Hill Book Co., 1966), 5-6 and in William D. McLoughlin, Jr., *Billy Graham* (New York: Ronald Press, 1960), 27-29.

14. Quoted in Norman Grubb, C. T. *Studd* (Atlantic City, N.J.: World Wide Prayer Movement, 1935), 49.

15. C. T. Studd, quoted in "A Sure Foundation," *Worldwide* (March-April 1964).

16. This is the substance of my paper read at the World Congress on Evangelism in Berlin, published in *One Race, One Gospel, One Task*, vol. 2, 210-12.

17. *Sanctification* means "to set apart" for God and hence to make holy. The context determines how the word is to be applied. In this instance, it relates to the preparation necessary for the fulfillment of Christ's mission in the world. The work of the Spirit in the lives of disciples is to make them a blessing to the world. As Paul put it: "Useful to the Master and prepared to do any good work" (2 Timothy 2:21 NIV). For further discussion on the ministry of the Holy Spirit, see my book, *The Mind of the Master* (Old Tappan, N.J.: Fleming H. Revell, 1977), 21-36.

18. Charles Spurgeon, quoted in *Worldwide* (January-February, 1959): 7.

Three

The Pattern of Renewal in the Bible

S PIRITUAL RENEWAL SHAPES THE REDEMPTIVE ACTIVITY of the Holy Spirit throughout the Bible. Tracing this stream of life is like listening to a person's heartbeat; it sounds the deep craving of our soul, which will rise to assert itself when given a chance. But is there a discernible pattern to such renewal in the Bible? A broad view of the inspired narrative will help us answer this question.[1]

Early Lessons About Renewal

The story of spiritual renewal begins with Genesis. What might be called the first general awakening occurred in the days of Seth shortly after the birth of his son Enos. "Then began men to call upon the name of the Lord" (Genesis 4:26).

Significantly the name Enos means feeble or sickly. Considering that this account follows the murder of Abel

(Genesis 3:9-15) and looking at the growing evidence of disease in the human race, one can easily see why such a name was appropriate. It probably reflects an awareness of human depravity and the need for grace.

Apart from this one allusion, there is no record of any great awakening in the early history of Adam's race. People lived long in those days, and their families were prolific, but with the exception of Enoch, there seems to be no corresponding fruitfulness in the things of God. This may explain why conditions in the world eventually deteriorated to the point that "the Lord was grieved that he had made man on the earth" (Genesis 6:6 NIV).

The subsequent account of the flood dramatically illustrates what happens to a sinful people when the call to revival is unheeded (Genesis 6:1–7:22). Noah, "a righteous man, blameless among the people of his time" (Genesis 6:9 NIV), was called a "preacher of righteousness" (2 Peter 2:5), which suggests that he warned his generation of God's impending judgment. Though the Spirit sought to bring conviction to the rebellious people for 120 years, it does not appear that they wanted to repent. Finally God gave them up to destruction.

Likewise, the wicked inhabitants of Sodom and Gomorrah scorned revival in their day. Abraham pleaded with God on their behalf, but not ten people were found who could meet the agreed-upon condition of personal righteousness (Genesis 18:14-19).

It is noteworthy that in both of these incidents, cited by Jesus as examples of God's judgment (Matthew 24:37-39; 10:15), ample warning was given before the final execution of justice. Certainly they are graphic reminders that, though

God is longsuffering, there comes a time when His patience is exhausted. Ultimately it is either revival or catastrophe. We can be grateful that during those fearful days of judgment there were some persons, such as Noah and Abraham, whose obedience to God was beyond reproach and who thereby preserved a posterity for the Lord.

Leadership of the Fathers

For several centuries the patriarchs gave leadership to God's people. And whenever spiritual vitality languished, they were the rallying force for renewal. The brief revival in Jacob's house is a good example (Genesis 35:1-15). In this instance, the shameful behavior of Jacob's children among the Shechemites had created a situation in which the house of Israel faced annihilation by their enraged neighbors (Genesis 34:1-31). Destruction seemed certain. But Jacob, the spokesman for God, rose to the occasion. He commanded that his household put away their strange gods, purify themselves, and go back to Bethel, the place where the blessing of the Lord had seemed so real. Though the repentance of his children was short-lived, and Jacob's own example was rather careless (cf. Genesis 35:4, 16), still it served to keep alive the chosen race.

However, the era of the godly patriarchs runs its course. After the death of Joseph, no strong leadership comes forth. With the passing of the friendly Pharaohs, the Israelites find themselves bereft of spiritual inspiration within and afflicted by cruel taskmasters without.

For hundreds of years the children of Israel languish in this bondage. Yet in their suffering they at last remember

God, their help in ages past. Somehow their tears turn into prayers: "And their cry came up unto God by reason of the bondage. And God heard their groaning, and God remembered his covenant with Abraham, with Isaac and with Jacob" (Exodus 2:23-24).

As usually happens in such situations, God answers prayer by raising up a shepherd for His people (Exodus 3:1-22). Under the leadership of Moses there are some exciting seasons of refreshing, particularly in the events surrounding the first Passover (Exodus 12:21-28), the giving of the Law at Sinai (Exodus 19:1-25; 24:1-8; 32:1-35:29), and the lifting up of the brazen serpent at Mount Hur (Numbers 21:4-9). But as so often before, the people soon forget their vows and turn their backs on God. The only stabilizing influence in the nation is Moses and the few faithful men gathered around him.

Periodic Awakenings

As the ungrateful people perish in the wilderness, God raises up a new generation, and Joshua is called to lead them into the promised land. For the most part a spiritual enthusiasm pervades their campaigns, as in the crossing of the river Jordan (Joshua 3:1-5:12) and the conquest of Ai (Joshua 7:1-8:35). However, after the wars end and the people settle down to enjoy the spoils of victory, a spiritual apathy creeps over the nation. Knowing that his people are divided, Joshua gathers the tribes of Israel at Shechem and demands that everyone choose once and for all whom they will serve (Joshua 24:1-32). A real revival follows this challenge, which continues "throughout the lifetime of Joshua and of the elders who outlived him and who had experienced everything the Lord had done for Israel" (Joshua 24:31 NIV).

The three-hundred-year period of rule by judges shows the Israelites again and again forsaking the Lord and serving other gods. Judgment inevitably follows. Then, after long years of oppression, the people repent and cry to God for help (Judges 3:9, 15; 4:3; 6:6-7; 10:10). Each time God answers their prayer by sending a deliverer who leads the people in conquest of their enemy. The greatest of these movements comes at the close of the era under the judgeship of Samuel (1 Samuel 7:1-17).

Times of renewal come periodically during the age of the kings. David's march into Jerusalem with the Ark has many ingredients of a spiritual awakening (2 Samuel 6:12-23). The dedication of the temple in the early reign of Solomon approaches the same spirit (1 Kings 8:1-65). Revival comes to Judah in the days of Asa (1 Kings 15:9-15). Jehoshaphat leads a reformation (1 Kings 22:41-50), as does Jehoiada (2 Kings 11:4-12:16). A mighty awakening is savored in the land under the leadership of King Hezekiah (2 Kings 18:1-8). Finding the Book of the Law precipitates renewal during Josiah's rule (2 Kings 22:1-23:30).

It is interesting that all of these revivals center in the southern kingdom of Judah. The nearest thing to a national awakening among the northern tribes comes at Mount Carmel when Elijah triumphs over the prophets of Baal (1 Kings 18:1-46). This victory is short-lived and not repeated, which doubtless is the reason why the beleaguered ten tribes crumble 150 years sooner than the little kingdom to the south. Nevertheless, even in Judah conditions rapidly deteriorate following Josiah's reign. When no revival comes to avert God's wrath, the children of Israel are conquered and carried away into captivity.

Bondage again brings the Jews to their knees, and God moves upon the king of Persia to send the Israelites back to Jerusalem to rebuild the temple. Under the leadership of Zerubbabel and Jeshua revival fires begin to burn (Ezra 1:1-4:24). When harassment causes the Jews to quit their task, the prophets Haggai and Zechariah stir up the people to keep on (Ezra 5:1-6:22; Haggai 1:1-2:23; Zechariah 1:1-21; 8:1-23). Seventy-five years later, with the coming of another expedition to Judah led by Ezra, new reforms are initiated and more attention is given to the law (Ezra 7:1-10:44). The revival reaches its climax a few years later when Nehemiah arrives to finish the building of the walls of Jerusalem and establishes a holy government (Nehemiah 1:1-13:31).

The Hope of Israel Kept Alive

These periods of reformation were the high peaks of corporate worship in the life of Israel. God's chosen people rallied around their own heritage of holiness. And by the beauty of their holy lifestyle the Gentile world was drawn to worship their God. This was the divine strategy of evangelism throughout the Old Testament.[2]

Unfortunately, the revivals usually lacked depth and permanence. They never completely erased the tendency toward rebellion.[3] It would appear that expediency more often than not dictated the people's choice. When religious devotion was expected of them by their leaders, the people complied; but when the pressure was off, they took the path of least resistance.

The Old Testament stream of authentic revival flowed largely in the hearts of a few people who bore the burden of the Lord. Even in times of national apostasy, there was a faithful remnant who would not capitulate to evil. In their experience with God, they kept alive the hope of that special nation through which Immanuel would bring salvation to the world.

Revival at the Coming of Jesus

In the fullness of time the promised Savior does appear. He lives for thirty years in relative obscurity. Then, as the time draws near for His public ministry to begin, suddenly a mighty prophet comes calling upon the people to repent: "Prepare the way for the Lord. . . . After me will come one who is more powerful than I, whose sandals I am not fit to carry. He will baptize you with the Holy Spirit and with fire" (Matthew 3:1-12 NIV).

A revival such as Israel had not seen in four hundred years begins to sweep across the land. As the excitement reaches its height, Jesus appears in the midst of the awakening and is baptized by John. There He is identified by the prophet as "the Lamb of God, who takes away the sin of the world" (John 1:29 NIV; cf. 1:36). Then the voice of God speaks from heaven, saying, "'You are my Son, whom I love; with you I am well pleased'" (Mark 1:11 NIV).

Having now accomplished its special purpose, the movement centered in John the Baptist fades away while the ministry of Christ quickly moves into prominence. At this point one might expect Jesus to seize the opportunity to proclaim Himself king and establish a rule of righteousness by decree.

Certainly the opportunity is ripe for a great popular revolution. The people are fed up with the oppressions of Rome. They are eager to have their stomachs full and their national pride satisfied.

Yet the movement that begins to gather around Jesus takes a different course. Contrary to the pattern seen so often before, the Son of God does not seek the immediate following of the masses. Rather, in His infinite understanding of the human problem, He concentrates His attention upon a few men destined to be the nucleus of a Spirit-filled church.

The Problem of the Multitudes

Of course, large crowds do attend Jesus' public services, sometimes numbering into the thousands (see Mark 6:44; Matthew 14:4; Luke 9:14; John 6:10). He instructs them. He feeds them. He heals them. Indeed, His deeds of mercy are so genuine that "everyone" clamors for His attention (John 3:26). Once the people want to "take him by force, to make him a king" (John 6:15). The enthusiasm with which the masses greet Jesus certainly indicates that the fields are ripe for harvest (Mark 1:14–6:9; John 4:1-47; Luke 13:22–19:28).

Had Jesus given any encouragement to this popular sentiment, He could easily have enlisted a vast army and taken the country by storm. He needed only to satisfy the fleshly appetites of the people by His miraculous power, and He could have had the world at His feet. For the first time in history a great welfare state where everyone's physical needs could be indulged appeared to be within reach.

In all honesty we must ask: Why doesn't Jesus do it? Why

doesn't He use His invincible power to overthrow all His enemies and establish a society that would never again know suffering or pain? That was the kind of Messiah the people were looking for—someone who would satisfy every temporal desire for personal pleasure and security.

But Jesus had a greater objective in view. He had not come to receive the superficial plaudits of the self-centered multitudes; He came to save a people from sin and to build a holy Church against which the gates of hell could not prevail. So Jesus chose to concentrate His life upon developing character and vision in a relatively small group of disciples. He knew that before the Gospel could effect a lasting change in the world, some laborers had to be raised up who could lead the multitudes in the things of God.[4]

What good would it have done for Jesus to have aroused a great mass following without laying a foundation to assure their spiritual nurture? Time and time again it had been demonstrated that the crowd fell easy prey to false gods when left without proper care. The masses were like sheep without a shepherd (Mark 6:34). They were willing to follow almost anyone who came along with some promise for their welfare, be it friend or foe. That was the tragedy of the hour—the noble aspirations of the people were easily excited by Jesus, but just as quickly thwarted by the cold religious establishment that controlled them (John 8:44; 9:39-41; 12:40).

The Master's Plan

Jesus is a realist. He knows full well the fickleness of depraved human nature, as well as the satanic forces of this world. And in this knowledge He follows a plan that will meet the need. The opportunity for a great national awakening is present, but Jesus individually cannot possibly give to all the people the personal care needed to nurture the fruit of revival. His plan is to raise up men and women who can multiply His ministry and to imbue them with His love and vision for the world. Though He does all He can to help the multitudes, He devotes Himself primarily to training a few in order that the masses can at last be reached.

It is this practical concern that characterizes Jesus' approach to revival and directs the Church about Him. Revival in Jesus' ministry has much the same purpose as in Old Testament times, but preservation is given a new emphasis. While Jesus plants and cultivates seeds of revival in the present, He is always preparing a band of disciples to reap the harvest in generations to come.

Jesus' method of training this vanguard is simply to draw them together around Himself.[5] He doesn't establish a formal school, nor does He prescribe a creed. He simply asks His disciples to follow Him. His teaching is incarnated in His own person. By following Him they know the truth, the way, and the life. As they grow in self-confidence and skill, He involves them in work assignments suited to their gifts, and He checks on them to see how they are coming along.

After three years of ministering with His disciples, Jesus sends them forth to make disciples of others (Matthew 28:19). They could understand what He meant, for they had seen the Great Commission lived out before their eyes. Just as He had discipled them, now they were asked to go and do likewise.

But before He leaves them, He assures them of His continuing presence (Matthew 28:20). "Another Comforter," one in quality like Himself, will come to take His place in their midst (John 14:16). In the strength of this ever-present Counselor, they will be enabled to continue the ministry Christ had begun. Though the Spirit had always been at work in the world, Jesus promises that they will now experience His presence in a measure hitherto unknown to them (John 14:1–16:33).

It is easy to see why Jesus expects His disciples to tarry until this promise is realized. How else could they fulfill the Great Commission? The evangels of His church must be obsessed with their Lord. His compassion for a lost world and His dedication to the work of God must become a burning compulsion within them. This can become a reality only as they are filled with His Spirit. Having enunciated this truth clearly, the glorified Jesus ascends into heaven, leaving His expectant disciples waiting for the promised outpouring (Luke 24:49-53; Acts 1:1-26).

Revival at Pentecost

The mighty infilling of the Holy Spirit at Pentecost inaugurates the revival for which Jesus had been preparing (Acts 2:1-47). It marks the beginning of a new era in the history of redemption. For three years He had been working for this day—the day when His church, trained by His example, redeemed by His blood, assured by His resurrection, would go forth in His name to proclaim the Gospel "unto the uttermost part of the earth" (Acts 1:8).[6]

As the Spirit-anointed witnesses declare "the wonderful

works of God" to all who will hear, the multitudes stand in wonder before them (Acts 2:6-13). When Peter explains what it is all about and invites the people to believe on Christ, about three thousand receive the word and are baptized (Acts 2:41). What is more, they continue to grow in the life of their new-found Lord (Acts 2:42). Brotherly concern (Acts 2:44), generosity (Acts 2:45), and unity of spirit characterize their life together (Acts 2:46). The love of God fills their souls with praise (Acts 2:46-47). Miracles happen (Acts 2:43). As the people look on in amazement, they can see that something has made a difference. God is real! "And the Lord added to the church daily such as should be saved" (Acts 2:47).

What happens on the day of Pentecost is only a foretaste of what is to come. The revival continues to spread across the city of Jerusalem. Daily—in the temple, in the streets, and in their houses "great power" and "great grace was upon them all" (Acts 4:33). Before long thousands are converted, including many of the Jewish priests (Acts 4:4; 6:1, 7). Their faith is attested to by works of love. Freely they give of their substance to care for the poor (Acts 4:34-37). With the same compassion, they believe for the healing of the sick (Acts 3:1-11; 5:12-16). And within their fellowship is a wonderful oneness of heart and soul (Acts 4:32; 5:12).

Difficulties Overcome

Yet they have their problems. One couple among them, Ananias and Sapphira, are deceitful in their profession (Acts 5:1-10). Whenever this many people get together, there are likely to be some who do not belong. But the way God judges these hypocrites only serves to draw the church closer together in holiness and to bring more people from the out-side to believe on Christ (Acts 5:11-14).

There is the problem, too, of a few Greek-speaking widows who feel that they are being neglected by the Hebrews in the daily ministration. When this situation is brought to the atten-tion of the apostles, they wisely call a congregational meeting to discuss the matter. Out of this discussion they decide to insti-tute the order of deacons to assist in the administration of the local church (Acts 6:1-6). Again the way the problem is handled enhances the reputation of the Christian community, and the number of disciples greatly multiplies in Jerusalem (Acts 6:7). Problems confronted by the church in the glow of revival become stepping stones to greater spiritual progress.[7]

We must not assume, however, that the Christians have it easy. Most of the time they witness under the threat of pun-ishment by the ruling aristocracy (Acts 4:1-31; 5:17-42). They are beaten. They are imprisoned. One of their leaders, Stephen, is stoned to death (Acts 6:8–7:60). Yet their adversi-ties never restrain their zeal or temper their joy. In fact, they rejoice that they are counted worthy to suffer shame for Jesus' sake (Acts 5:41). The persecutions succeed only in scattering the revival across the land, for wherever the Christians flee, they carry with them the spirit of Pentecost (Acts 8:1-4; 11:19). Even the martyrdom of Stephen contributes to the conversion of Saul, the chief persecutor of the church (Acts 8:1; 9:1-31).[8]

The Revival Spreads

As the years move on, the revival continues to spread. Not everything that happens is reported, of course. But it is significant that the events that *are* reported show the spirit of revival attending each breakthrough of the Gospel into new regions. It moves into Samaria where the first congregation is raised up outside the Jewish nation (Acts 8:5-25).[9] The revival reaches into the house of Cornelius at Caesarea, which marks the beginning of the work among Gentile believers (Acts 10:1–11:18; 15:7-28).[10] The same spirit brings together a congregation of both Jews and Gentiles at Antioch (Acts 11:19-30). As this church becomes well established, the Spirit speaks to their listening hearts, and two of their staff are sent out as missionaries to the world (Acts 13:1-4). Thereafter the action shifts to the exploits of Paul as he bears the Gospel witness to the ends of the earth.

Following the Spirit's leading, the missionaries begin work in each new city by going to the most likely place to find spiritually hungry people—usually the synagogue. There they present the claims of Christ and draw out those the Spirit has prepared. From this nucleus a congregation is established and their own people trained for leadership. In turn these new Christians evangelize the surrounding area until "the word of the Lord was published throughout all the region" (Acts 13:49; 19:20, 26; 1 Thessalonians 1:8-9). The harvests at Antioch in Pisidia (Acts 13:14-52), Philippi (Acts 16:12-40), Thessalonica (Acts 17:1-9; 1 Thessalonians 1:8-9), and Ephesus (Acts 18:19–19:41; 20:17-38) are especially interesting to study.

Acts reads like one long narrative of Pentecost. Nothing can stop these new believers—not the anger of mobs or the irritations of daily trials—but as rivers borne along with a loud rushing sound, they go on their way praising God and scattering abroad the seed of the Gospel. Although some local congregations lose the vision that gave them birth,[11] and doubtless many individual Christians fall below their privileges in the Spirit-filled life, nevertheless the New Testament Church as a whole maintains a remarkable fervency of spirit and an outreach of love. Something about them makes the world aware "that they had been with Jesus" (Acts 4:13). In their lives the living Christ is lifted up, and as men and women see Him, revival spreads from the center to the circumference in the power of the Holy Spirit.

The Acts of the Apostles has no close. It simply breaks off the narrative by reporting that "preaching the kingdom of God, and teaching those things which concern the Lord Jesus Christ" continued with "all confidence . . . " (Acts 28:31). That is the way the New Testament leaves the record of revival. There is no finish. And, indeed, wherever the true spirit of Pentecost prevails in any age, there will be no end to revival.

Study Assignments 3

Personal Study

1. Read the climactic account of the great post-exilic revival in Nehemiah 8:1–13:31. As you think again about the reasons for this revival, what principles do you see in the story?

What effect does obedience to God's Word have upon the worship of the people (12:43)?

According to Nehemiah 9:28, what is the pattern leading to revival?

2. Read the story of Jehoshaphat's reign in 2 Chronicles 17:1–21:1, giving particular attention to the events recorded in chapters 19 and 20. How did the king lead his people in responding to the invasion of the land by a powerful enemy?

How did the king lead his people in responding to the Word of God through the prophet Jahaziel?

What was unusual about the way the Jews went into battle?

How did the king lead his people in accepting God's victory?

Generally the twenty-five-year reign of Jehoshaphat was marked by religious devotion, yet some evident weaknesses led to spiritual deterioration as soon as the king died. What were they? Note 2 Chronicles 20:33, 35-37 (18:1–19:3); 21:1-6.

3. As you see it now, what is the basic problem in perpetuating revival in the Old Testament?

4. With this in mind, do you see a contrast with the pattern of revival in Jesus' ministry? If so, what is it?

5. In what sense does Pentecost form the pattern of revival in the Acts of the Apostles?

6. Reviewing your experience in the church, how would you say that the Spirit-filled life of Pentecost has dominated your congregation?

7. How do you see your own spiritual development during these years? Do you recognize any difference between your experience and that of the Church in general? Wherever you place your present experience in the over-all pattern of the congregation, what are you doing to help the situation?

Group Discussion

As you meet again in your group, center the discussion on the pattern of revival in the Bible. Why does it ebb and flow all through the Old Testament? Why did Jesus take the course He did? In what sense can Pentecost be called Jesus' revival? Your answers to the "Personal Study" questions will open up the subject; then let the group take it from there. When you share your interpretation of questions six and seven, you will probably receive some varied responses. Let each person explain his or her view. This will lead you to some conclusions that can direct your closing prayer.

Option of Continuing Study

Perhaps you would like to spend more time studying the biblical accounts of revival. If there is this interest, the references to revival noted in this chapter will point you to the most important accounts.

Read each revival account at one sitting. Try to get the feel of the situation. Then go back over it, asking questions to bring out the meaning of the text. Record your impressions, noting any matters you would like to explore further.

In each account observe the conditions showing the need for revival. When did the events take place? What were the social and economic circumstances of the people? Were they prosperous? Poor? Depressed? What was the political situation? Was the nation entangled in unholy alliances? Was there some great national crisis threatening their security? What was the condition of the religious leaders? How did the people reflect the problem? Was there disregard for the law? Covenants broken? Indifference to worship and sacrifice? Ignorance of the Scriptures? Prayerlessness? Self-containment? How long had it been since the last revival?

Once the overall problem is in view, observe how God sought to meet the need by raising up concerned leadership. Who was the human instrument through which the people were challenged? How was this person qualified? Early training? Personality? Devotion to God? Knowledge of the Scriptures? How many others were faithful? Why had these persons become burdened? What was the central message God laid on their hearts? How was it presented to the people? Was a decision demanded? What gave the call a sense of urgency? Consider then what happened in response to the challenge. Did many follow the leader? In what way? Prayer? Fasting? Confession? False altars torn down? Restitution? Scriptures studied? Obedience to the law? Sacrifices offered? House of worship restored? Was the revival progressive or sudden? In what sense?

What spiritual and material benefits came to the people? Cleansing? Unity? Healing of sickness? Protection from evil? Prosperity? How was the revival spirit expressed in their feeling of gladness? Spontaneous praise to God? Singing? Generosity of gifts?

What social good resulted from the new spirit? What effect did the revival have upon neighboring people? Was there opposition to the movement? How did it come and what was its effect? How lasting was the revival?

This last question may lead to some interesting insights concerning the decline of spiritual movements, particularly in the Old Testament. When did the revival begin to lose its vision? Why were the people frustrated in their aspirations and vows? Was repentance superficial to begin with? Did they become complacent in their blessings? Had they received adequate nurture and training in their faith? What was it? What happened to their spiritual leadership? Why were not other leaders raised up to take their place? In spite of the recoil, how was the true worship of God still kept alive?

As you analyze the course of each revival, compare it with other movements in the Bible. What did it have in common with similar awakenings? In what way did it differ? Summing up your whole study, what is the most significant lesson you have learned?

Not all your questions will be answered, but this method

of inductive study will bring you to some conclusions about the origin and course of great revivals. Further study will gradually crystalize in your mind principles underlying these movements. Note the application of these patterns to your situation today. The study of biblical revivals can have a meaningful impact on your life.

NOTES

1. While no amount of reading in the other sources can substitute for a direct confrontation with Scripture itself, the student may find it helpful to consult secondary materials where available. The best study available now specifically dealing with revivals in the Old Testament is the recent book by Walter C. Kaiser, Jr., *Quest for Renewal* (Chicago: Moody Press, 1986). To this could be added the previously cited treatment of C. E. Autrey, *Revivals of the Old Testament* (Grand Rapids: Zondervan, 1960). Both Old and New Testament revivals are considered in less detail by Ernest Baker in *Great Revivals of the Bible* (London: The Kingsgate Press, 1906). Some selected studies are also available, such as Wilbur M. Smith's little book, *The Glorious Revival Under King Hezekiah* (Grand Rapids: Zondervan, 1954). Of course, commentaries and histories of the two Testaments will allude to revivals in the course of their interpretation of Scripture, and sometimes these accounts are rich with insights. However, the need is apparent for more scholarly and creative work in this area, and a definitive study encompassing the whole Bible has yet to be written.

2. This design to reach the world can be seen in the call of Abraham to leave his pagan society in Ur and go out with God to raise up a holy people: "I will make you into a great nation and I will bless you; I will make your name great, and you will be a blessing. . . . And all peoples on earth will be blessed through you" (Genesis 12:1-3 NIV; cf. 17:1-8; 22:15-18). Here the mandate of the Great Commission begins in the call to holiness with its inevitable outreach to the peoples of the earth. The life of revival is at its heart. Though direct evangelization of the pagan world is not given emphasis in the Old Testament revivals, the principle is always present.

However, there is the story of Jonah's mission to Nineveh, which results in something of an awakening in that heathen city (Jonah 1:1-4:11). Clearly from the onset God's compassion was not limited to the Jews. But for the sake of His purpose of world evangelism, the Spirit's work narrows upon the chosen race through whom in the Messiah redemption will come to all nations.

3. There is an undercurrent of rebellion all through the history of Israel (Jeremiah 3:25; 8:5; Zechariah 1:4-6; Acts 7:51-53). Revival times may check this

condition, but it is still there to assert itself when given a chance (for example, note Isaiah 65:1-3 in reference to Hezekiah's reign, or Jeremiah 3:6-11, which alludes to Josiah's era). This may remind us of the law serving as a schoolmaster to bring us to Christ. It may also underscore the need for more depth in follow up to popular renewal movements.

4. This whole section on Jesus' ministry is taken from my book, *The Master Plan of Evangelism* (Westwood, N.J.: Fleming H. Revell, 1964), 22-35. The principles of evangelism outlined in this book form the basis for much of my thinking about revival. I believe that the way Jesus went about His ministry in principle is the way that all of us should pattern our lives, and this includes our work for revival. How this relates to our daily conduct is described in my book, *The Great Commission Lifestyle* (Grand Rapids: Revell/Baker, 1992).

5. Jesus' strategy of training disciples in the context of a small spiritual family was not new. It was God's plan from the beginning. Formal religious instruction and worship grew out of the home and was never intended to replace the home's central religious role. This was clearly enunciated by Moses in the Law (Deuteronomy 4:9; 6:7; 21:19; 31:13). The responsibility to train up children by precept and example clearly rested upon the parents. Sadly, it would appear that these responsibilities were largely transferred to formal institutions throughout Old Testament times. But in His own ministry Jesus revived the central role of the home.

6. For a discussion of the pattern of Jesus' lifestyle in the New Testament Church, see my book, *The Master Plan of Discipleship* (Old Tappan, N.J.: Fleming H. Revell, 1987). In this study of the book of Acts, the principles of the Great Commission in Christ's ministry are now seen to take contextualized form in His rapidly growing Church.

7. A rapid increase in church membership, as happened in the Jerusalem church, invariably precipitates problems. There is always the danger of some coming into the movement who are superficial in their commitment, as happened with Ananias and Sapphira. Also, when numbers swell the size of a congregation, administrative functions can be sorely taxed, as in the case of the murmuring widows. Other problems arose too—the greed of Simon (Acts 8:9-24), the hesitancy of the church to forgive and accept the converted Saul (Acts 9:26), legalism (Acts 11:10-18, 15:1-35), friction between ministers (Acts 13:13; 15:36-40), and fear (Acts 21:12). Revival does not prevent all conflicts, but it does give spiritual stamina to overcome them. A helpful discussion of this matter is in C. E. Autrey, *Evangelism in the Acts* (Grand Rapids: Zondervan, 1964), 43-78.

8. Notwithstanding the currently popular "comfort-and-prosperity" teaching, suffering was inherent in the apostolic lifestyle, and it contributed vitally to church growth. Note my chapter on discipline in *The Master Plan of Discipleship*, 98-118.

9. It is worthy of note that the first penetration of the Gospel outside the Jewish world of that day comes in the same area where a few years before there had been a remarkable response to Jesus' ministry (John 4:39-42). Doubtless the message of Christ was not altogether new to these people, and very likely some in the area

already were believers. I cannot help but observe the principle of beginning where the greatest spiritual preparation occurs.

10. Again we note the pattern of beginning with those whose hearts are already yearning for spiritual reality. Cornelius and his house were probably the most sensitive people in the Gentile world at that time. Though their understanding of truth was limited, still they were walking in all the light they had. When they received the more complete revelation through the apostle, their hearts immediately responded.

11. Indications of this are seen in some of the letters of Paul—for example, Corinthians. The book of Revelation also speaks of various church problems. One church mentioned is Ephesus, a church that earlier had known real revival (Revelation 2:1-7). Pergamos, Thyatira, Sardis, and Laodicea are other churches mentioned as being in need (Revelation 2:12–3:6; 14:22).

Four

The Spark That Ignites: Church Renewal Today

W E BELIEVE THE SPIRIT-FILLED REALITY OF PENTE-cost to be the norm for the church; but when it is not, what course of action can we follow to experience revival? Do the patterns of revival in the Bible offer any guidelines for church renewal today?

"Men [and Women] Are God's Method"

Revival, like any spiritual reality, involves human personality. As E. M. Bounds puts it, "Men are God's method."[1] Programs, techniques, campaigns, and the like are utterly useless unless the people who work the schemes are under the control of the Holy Spirit.

The call is to obedience—to follow Jesus whatever the cost. God is looking for people who will let themselves go and dare to be fools for Christ.[2] Dawson Trotman put it

bluntly, "God can do more through one man who is 100 percent dedicated to him than through a hundred men 90 percent dedicated to him."[3] Half-hearted, weak-kneed,
compromising obedience will never challenge a sleeping
church to rise up and rescue perishing souls from the jaws
of hell. Highly sophisticated church members may look upon
such unfettered zeal for Christ as fanaticism. But it is still the
way the Spirit works in revival.

A German pastor once aroused his lethargic congregation by suddenly exclaiming, "Fire! Fire! Fire!"

"Where?" the startled congregation asked.

He answered, "In disciples' hearts."[4]

To be sure, that is where revival fires start—in the hearts
of God's people (Hebrews 1:7). Are we combustible material? Has the promised baptism with the Holy Spirit and with
fire become a reality? Would that each of us could be as Jim
Elliot when he prayed, "God deliver me from the dread
asbestos of other things. Saturate me with the oil of the
Spirit that I may be aflame. . . . Father, take my life, yea, my
blood if Thou wilt, and consume it with Thine enveloping
fire. I would not save it, for it is not mine to save. Have it,
Lord, have it all. . . . Pour out my life as an oblation for the
world. . . . Make me Thy fuel, Flame of God!"[5]

You Be That Person!

Is not this the reasonable service of every Christian? Of
course, it is logical to expect the church officials to lead the
way. However, the burden for revival should not rest only
with these leaders, nor should it be thought essential to bring
in leadership from the outside. Every member of the con-

gregation should look upon revival as a personal responsibility and find the place of service most suited to his or her talents and personality.

The time has come to quit ascribing the problem to other people in the church. What about you? Regardless of your position in the church and whatever gifts you may possess, have you fulfilled the conditions for revival in your own life? Are you completely open to the Spirit's direction? Is your heart cleansed from every evil desire and selfish purpose? Mere concern for revival is not enough. Is your heart, your home, your business a witness to the overflowing love of God?

Face it! As fully as you know your will and as fully as you know the will of God, can you say that there is no competition? If not, you are still part of the problem.

Samuel Chadwick, the beloved principal of Cliff College and peer among English preachers, tells how he started his ministry infatuated with his own eloquence as a speaker. Taking a pastorate in a little Lancashire cotton town, he fully expected his preaching to bring a revival to the church. But nothing happened.

One Saturday night as he was going over his notes for his sermon, God revealed to him his sinful egotism. He had believed that his strength lay in his ability to preach, and he had forgotten that God alone is the source of all blessing. There was an agonizing struggle. It went on past the midnight hour. As the young preacher sought the face of God, all he could hear was, "Burn those sermons." Finally at three o'clock in the morning he kindled a fire in the kitchen grate and burned the sermons. As the flames consumed his elegant notes, it seemed that a new fire was kindled in his heart.

Revival had come, and the next day the young preacher witnessed the beginning of a mighty awakening in his church.[6]

Until such leadership appears, there is little hope for the congregation. The church must be given in some individual life an example of what revival means. Someone must show the love of God bursting forth in redemptive concern for the world; the beauty of holiness must be incarnated in human personality. People respond to a *demonstration* of revival, not an *explanation*. You be that person!

Find the Committed Nucleus

One person burning with the love of God invariably ignites another. It is the nature of fire not only to consume, but also to spread. As the divine spark leaps from heart to heart, more and more people see the inadequacy of nominal religion, and the cry for revival rises with increasing frequency. Gradually out of this growing concern a nucleus emerges that desires revival at any cost.

Look around you for these people. As God has dealt with you, He has surely spoken to others. Like yourself, they are seeking God's best. The shallow religion of our day has not deceived their spirit. They know that there are deeper riches in God's Word, and they are open to the Spirit's instruction.

Likely such a group is waiting for direction right now in your church. They may be unorganized, perhaps not even aware of their mutual desires, but they are there. And they only need encouragement and leadership to become a dynamic force for revival. Do not worry if their numbers are few. Jesus started with just a handful. Any spiritual movement begins with the committed few who care.[7] History may give these small groups little notoriety; interest naturally focuses upon the larger movements that they foster and undergird.[8] Nevertheless, the dynamic of revival lies in these small clusters of earnest souls.

Find these concerned people who want revival. Discover what you can do together to stimulate your faith and enlarge your ministry. You do not need to break off other contacts to have this association. In fact, to give your witness an effective outlet, you must hold on to and enlarge your friendships in the church and community. But in your continuing witness through the ongoing program of the larger congregation, you dare not ignore your need to develop this potential nucleus of revival. The fallacy of so much church activity is that in our haste to rally the crowd, we neglect to cultivate the very people who ultimately must lead them.

Develop a Group Discipline

One of the most effective ways to help this nucleus grow is to meet regularly for fellowship, prayer, and Bible study. Two or three earnest souls are enough to start, though eight or nine makes a better number.

Since the group will not be bound by tradition, you can work out your own discipline in the light of your particular interests. In this close association of kindred spirits you can share with one another your burdens and desires. It is this family spirit that makes the small group approach so conducive to growth and gives it a depth of fellowship the larger public services of the church cannot provide.[9] Whatever form your group takes, at its heart should be a determination to seek God's purpose together.

The group members must be honest with God and with each other. It may take awhile to come to this freedom and trust. After all, you are not prone to bare your soul to people you do not know. But as you become united in love, do not fear to be your true self. Of course, this means you must keep faith with each other and never carry beyond the group matters shared in confidence.

The group must be careful, too, not to become complacent in its purpose. It is easy to level off on some plateau of experience and cease to press on to higher ground. Anytime you lose your sense of adventure, the door of progress closes. No matter what you have experienced thus far, more waits beyond.

A disciplined study in the deep things of God will help stretch your vision and dedication. There is no lack of helpful material to assist in this.[10] The important thing is to keep the study exciting and personally relevant. Be creative in your methods. If one approach begins to drag, try something new. Sometimes as a change of pace, you might read and discuss some provocative book or devotional classic.[11]

The group might occasionally have an overnight or weekend retreat to draw closer to God and to each other. It isn't difficult to find a suitable place. Sometimes more can be accomplished in a day on a retreat than in six months of meetings in the church.

The Outflow of the Inflow

But the group dare not become totally occupied with its own concerns.[12] The water of life should always be flowing out to bring healing to others. Anytime water becomes self-contained, it stagnates and is unfit to drink. As your fellowship drinks in deeply the love of God, a desire to minister to others should grow. Each member will want to find a practical way to do this.

The group can discuss this outreach together, not in theoretical terms, but in down-to-earth life experiences. In addition to encouraging individual witness, the group could adopt a cooperative service project such as a community visitation program, a witness mission to other churches, or an evangelistic neighborhood Bible study.

As group members give of themselves, the thrill of serving Christ overflows into the whole church. The influence of the group grows. New people want to join. Other groups want to start. And the experience and confidence gained by the nucleus will provide the reservoir of leadership for this growing fellowship.

Periodically a group should check up on itself to see if its purpose is being fulfilled. There is no point in doing anything merely for exercise. You may need occasionally to sharpen your discipline or change your form of meeting. The criteria for determining the value of any group always is its growth in the life and ministry of the Lord.

At times you may need to divide and start new groups with different combinations of people. There is no shame in division. In fact, the division itself may be an outreach of the group, for as the group divides, it forms the nucleus for other groups.

Mobilize the Church

With a group of dedicated people as a nucleus, the church as a whole can be inspired and directed in the service of Christ.

Of course, until this committed minority is present, there is
not much use talking about getting the larger congregation
involved. Before there can be followers, there must be leaders. But as the core of trained disciples grows and the various programs of the church are given more dynamic
direction, increasing numbers of people will see their own
spheres of ministry.

Total mobilization of the total church for the total ministry is the goal. Actually this is not an objective peculiar to
Christianity. It is a criterion of success in any enterprise, be
it business, government, the military, or evangelism. The
church should simply be as wise in utilizing her resources as
are the institutions of the world. "If our goal is the penetration of the whole world," observes Leighton Ford, "then . . .
we must aim at nothing less than the mobilization of the
whole church."[13]

Everyone Should Minister

The application of this principle has some revolutionary
implications. For one thing, it means that everyone who par-
ticipates in the life of Christ has a vital part in His plan for
the church.[14] Gifts and offices may differ, but each of us has
a unique function. "A church which bottlenecks its outreach
by depending upon its specialists—its pastors or evangelists—
to do its witnessing is living in violation of both the inten-
tion of its Head and the consistent pattern of the early
Christians."[15]

The distinction between clergy and laity does not appear
in the New Testament at all.[16] Moreover, the word *minister*,
as Elton Trueblood points out, "may be applied to anyone

who ministers, regardless of the secular mode of employ-ment."[17] This brings the concept of ministry into the daily life of mothers, factory workers, clerks, soldiers, farmers, stu-dents—every Christ-honoring vocation becomes a means of service and every location a place of witness.

Most of us find this concept hard to grasp. For example, as Richard Halverson observes:

> When we ask, "How many ministers does your church have?" the traditional answer is "one" or "two" or "five," depending upon how large the paid staff is. But the true answer is "two hundred" or "two thousand," depending on how large the membership is! Every believer is a minister! Or when we ask, "Where is your church?" the traditional reply is "on the corner of Broad and Main." But the correct reply is "What time is it?" If it's 11:00 A.M. Sunday, then my church is "on the corner of Broad and Main." (That's where the headquarters building is!) But if it's 11:00 A.M. Tuesday, then my church is in Room 511 in the Professional Building where Bill White, Christian attorney, is practicing law. It's at 3009 Melody Lane where Jane White, Christian house-wife, is making a home. It's at Central High where Jimmy White, Christian student, is studying to the glory of God. There is the Church in action![18]

What a difference it would make if we would start look-ing at the church ministry this way! Whatever our occupa-tion, it would be rendered as unto the Lord. Wherever we are, it would be a sanctuary of worship. Every day would be filled with the glory of God. This does not mean that the world automatically becomes holy because we are there, but it does say that we have the opportunity to witness in the world for Christ. It is in this sense that we are called and sent into the ministry (John 17:18; 20:21; Matthew 28:19-20).[19]

The church building is simply the "drill hall for the Christian task force."[20] It is the place where the soldiers come together to be trained, strengthened, and briefed in the art of warfare. The battle is not fought in the church. The battle is in the world, and church meetings are intended to prepare the church for the attack.

The Sparks That Ignited in China

What has been described in this strategy has been wonderfully illustrated in the awakening of the church in mainland China. When the missionaries were forced to leave China in 1951 and Christians began to be oppressed by the Communist government, the future of the church seemed bleak. In the preceding decades of Western missions work, many of the approximately one million Protestant communicants had become "rice Christians,"[21] accepting the forms of Christianity more for personal gain than out of genuine conviction. When the pressures began to mount, they soon fell away. With the coming of the Cultural Revolution and the suppression of all institutional religious functions, it seemed that Christianity in China was doomed.[22]

Yet during this period of terrible persecution, committed evangelical Christians, not afraid to defy the principalities of this world, began to meet secretly in their homes. When regular church services were outlawed during the "Great Leap Forward," these informal cottage meetings became the primary structure of the church. As their pastors were killed or imprisoned, members of the laity came forward to provide leadership. Women especially took an active role. When their houses were searched by the Red Guards and all Bibles and Christian literature destroyed, the people drew upon their memory of Scripture and shared experiences to build up one another in the faith.

As the Christians in these small groups displayed extraordinary courage, zeal, and love, the Gospel spread to their neighbors and fellow workers. Freely they gave their own food and clothing to the needy and poor—especially to those whose breadwinners had been killed or thrown into prison. They visited the bereaved and prayed for the sick, often seeing God miraculously heal.[23]

Typical was the way some believers cared for a Communist schoolteacher who became seriously ill. So genuine was their compassion that upon her recovery she, too, accepted Christ, only to suffer public ridicule on return to her work. Required to appear at a public "confession" meeting, she protested, "When I was ill, you did nothing to help me. It was the Christians who did everything!" The fact shamed her critics into silence.[24]

Such witnessing was not without cost. For more than three decades Christians in China have paid a price for their profession of faith. A letter from Henan Province in 1982 tells a story that could be repeated many times over. Ten young men and women went out to share their faith with passersby on the street. Soon a large crowd gathered to hear their joyful testimony. Learning of the meeting, security officials came, tied up the preachers, and beat them into unconsciousness.

> When one girl of only fourteen, after being beaten, revived
> and continued witnessing, all kinds of people broke down,
> repented and believed in Jesus. Four of the young men were
> arrested and forced to kneel for three days without food or
> water, but even as they were being beaten . . . they contin-
> ued praying, singing, and praising the Lord, until even
> their tormentors were convicted and believed the gospel.

The writer went on to say that in that locality "the flame of
the gospel has spread everywhere."[25]

Indeed, the flame has spread. Today the Christian community in China probably numbers seventy-five million
believers, a 7500 percent increase in little more than a generation! During much of this time Chinese Christians had
no church buildings, no colleges or seminaries, no access to
the media, no professional clergy, and were under constant
harassment by the state; but they had God—and they learned
through suffering the joy of obedience. In recent years official opposition to the church has somewhat subsided, and
some of the more traditional forms of public worship, ministerial training, and teaching are being widely reinstituted.[26]
If the present rate of growth continues, the potential outreach of the church in Asia is staggering to contemplate. But
whatever may happen in the future, the Christians in China,
without their Western connections, have shown us anew
what God can do when revival fires burn in the hearts of His
people.

Study Assignments 4

Personal Study

1. Read the account of revival under the leadership of Jehoiada the priest in 2 Chronicles 23:1–24:22. In a sentence or two, tell what you believe to be the greatest single reason for this awakening.

Sum up in a sentence why you feel the revival ceased. Note 24:14-19.

2. As you review the revivals in the Old Testament, do you recall any great spiritual movement that did not begin in dedicated leadership, and can you think of any that continued after spiritual leadership was gone?

Your answer to this question may help you appreciate more the way Jesus spent so much time training men to be shepherds in His church. Yet why do you suppose that Jesus developed only a comparatively small group of such men? Does this suggest anything to you about the practical requirements for dynamic teaching? Write a description of Jesus' method in developing a nucleus of revival.

3. Read carefully the account of the events leading up to Pentecost in Luke 24:49-53 and Acts 1:1–2:4. Why do you think Jesus insisted that His disciples tarry until they be endued with power from on high?

What were the expectant disciples doing while they waited

for the promised outpouring? Note especially the following verses: Luke 24:52; Acts 1:14; Acts 1:16.

What strikes you about their fellowship together? Note Acts 1:14; 2:1.

4. Read the account of the day of Pentecost in Acts 2. How many of the disciples were involved in the witness leading up to Peter's sermon?

When Peter gave an explanation of their witness (vv. 16-21) and then presented the claims of Christ (vv. 22-36), what effect did it have upon the people?

Following the great harvest of converts, how did the church maintain the revival spirit? Acts 2:42-47.

5. Read Acts 3 through 6, which describes something of the continuing experience of the Jerusalem church. How did the Christians respond to persecution from without? Note Acts 4:1-33; 5:17-42; 6:9-15; (7:1-60; 12:1-25).

How did they respond to urgent physical and social needs? Note Acts 3:1-26; 4:34-37; 5:12-16.

How did they respond to the mounting administrative problems in the church? Acts 6:1-8.

What was the place of the apostles in the developing structure of the church? Acts 6:4.

6. As you reflect upon the ministry of Christ multiplying through the disciples and in turn through their followers, how do you see this principle unfolding in your church? More specifically, how do you see it in your own life?

Group Discussion

Let your meeting this week really get at this matter of the dedicated minority leading the way for the larger congregation. Your study of revival to this point should have already focused on the subject. As you talk about it together, try to come up with some plans along this line for your church. Whatever strategy you visualize, find your place in the picture. The group may then make the implementation of these plans a focus for prayer.

NOTES

1. E. M. Bounds, *Power Through Prayer* (Chicago: Moody Press, 1979), 7.

2. This was a favorite expression of Paul in describing his own commitment. He was not saying that he was uneducated, for this was not the case. He was simply accepting the derision of the world as a compliment. Anytime one identifies with the Cross of Christ, both its theological content and its way of life, the world will call that person a fool. See 1 Corinthians 1:17–4:10; 2 Corinthians 11:23.

3. Dawson Trotman, quoted by Lorne Sanny in "The Adventure of a Yielded Life," *The Navigator's Log*, 113 (March/April 1967): 11.

4. Paulus Scharpff, *History of Evangelism* (Grand Rapids: Wm. B. Eerdmans, 1966), 118.

5. Jim Elliot, quoted in Elisabeth Elliot, *Shadow of the Almighty* (New York: Harper, 1958), 58-59, 240.

6. Told in the biography of Samuel Chadwick by Norman G. Dunning, *The Preacher as Prophet* (Athens: Georgia Bible Institute, n.d.), 12.

7. There are several examples in more recent history of small groups leading to larger revivals. These include the home Bible study meetings of the Pietist revival in Germany, the Holy Club in Wesley's experience, the class meetings of the evangelical revival in England and America, the student prayer meetings at Hampden-Sydney College in Virginia launching the second awakening in America, the noon-day meetings of the great midnineteenth-century revival, the haystack prayer meeting beginning the modern missionary movement, and the meetings of prayer and confession issuing in revivals in Wales, Korea, and Africa—to mention a few. An account of some contemporary forms of this

principle may be seen in David Prior's *Parish Renewal at the Grass Roots* (Grand Rapids: Francis Asbury Press of Zondervan, 1983).

8. The Billy Graham Crusades are a foremost example. Though the great public meetings receive the publicity, still much of the power behind a Graham crusade is generated in a whole network of small groups praying and working for the revival. Small groups also play an important role in crusade follow-up. Doubtless one of the greatest fruits of the Billy Graham ministry is the organization and encouragement of small groups of earnest disciples wherever crusades have been held.

9. There are many good books on how small groups work, including William Clemmons and Harvey Hester, *Growth Through Groups* (Nashville: Broadman Press, 1974); Ford Madison, *Small Groups: Together We Can Grow* (Wheaton, Ill.: Victor Books, 1980); Ralph W. Neighbor, Jr., *Where Do We Go from Here: A Guidebook for Cell Group Churches* (Houston, Tex.: Torch Publications, 1990); Steve Barker, Judy Johnson, Bob Malone, Ron Nicholes, Doug Whallon, *Good Things Come in Small Packages* (Downers Grove, Ill.: InterVarsity Press, 1985); and the simple story of this principle applied in the world's largest church, told by the pastor, Paul Y. Cho, *Successful Home Cell Groups* (Plainfield, N.J.: Logos, 1981). Excellent resources on small groups usually can be supplied through your own denominational publishing house or through para-church organizations such as The Navigators, Campus Crusade for Christ, the Billy Graham Evangelistic Association, Inter-Varsity Christian Fellowship, and Christian Outreach.

10. No one has developed any more creative programs in group Bible study than my brother, Lyman Coleman. His *Serendipity Bible for Groups* (1988) is a treasury of study courses for all kinds of people, complete with icebreakers, various levels of inductive questions, and personal applications. It offers enough to keep groups going for years. For adult personal and group study, his *Mastering the Basics* (1986) provides material based on several New Testament books. His *Youth Bible Study* series (1993), including a *Serendipity Youth Ministry Encyclopedia* (1994), features numerous group exercises to stimulate fellowship and study. These and many other materials designed for small groups may be ordered from Serendipity, Box 1012, Littleton, Colorado, 80160.

11. An example of a contemporary book that can be used in group discussion is *Knowing God* by J. I. Packer (Downers Grove, Ill.: InterVarsity Press, 1973). A study guide is available, too. Another book that lends itself well to group study is the author's *The Master Plan of Evangelism*. Dr. Roy Fish, Professor of Evangelism at Southwestern Baptist Seminary, has prepared a study guide for use with the book. Examples of devotional classics that offer stimulation in group study are Francois Fenelon, *Christian Perfection* (New York: Harper and Row, 1947); Andrew Murray, *Like Christ* (New York: Grosset and Dunlap, n.d.); and the book I have used more than any other, John Bunyan's, *Pilgrim's Progress*. I like especially the revised edition with notes by Warren W. Wiersbe, *The New Pilgrim's Progress* (Grand Rapids: Discovery House, 1989).

12. The group experience described here relates mainly to Christians. However, it could include anyone, provided the person is sincerely willing to seek the truth.

13. Leighton Ford, *The Christian Persuader* (Minneapolis: World Wide Publications, 1988), 45. Mobilizing laity for ministry and utilizing the gifts of the whole body are essential ingredients of church growth. For a brief review of this principle in evangelistic strategy, see C. Peter Wagner, *Strategies for Church Growth* (Ventura, Cal.: Regal Books, 1987), 138-50. A more complete discussion of the whole subject is Greg Ogden's *The New Reformation* (Grand Rapids: Zondervan, 1990).

14. For a forthright statement on what is expected of the laity in the church, read *Laymen: Look Up!* by Walter A. Henrichsen and William N. Garrison (Grand Rapids: Zondervan, 1983).

15. Ford, *Persuader*, 46.

16. It is significant that all of the disciples called by Jesus were laymen. They were not members of the officially recognized priesthood of their day. Not until sometime after Pentecost is there any indication that members of the clergy joined Christ's company (Acts 6:7). Of course Jesus ordained some of His disciples to positions of official leadership (Mark 3:14), as did the early church. But the ordination of these twelve did not negate the ministry of other believers, nor did it make the twelve a counterpart to the Old Testament priest.

17. Elton Trueblood, *The Incendiary Fellowship* (New York: Harper and Row, 1967), 39. Interestingly, the word in the New Testament from which "clergy" is derived normally translates "heir" or "inheritance," and when used in reference to the Church always includes the whole body of Christ. In the biblical sense, every believer belongs to the clergy—that is, when we are saved, we become "heirs" of Christ. See the note in Coleman, *The Master Plan of Discipleship*, 11.

18. Quoted by Leighton Ford, *Persuader*, 49.

19. It is in this sense that Christians are in the succession of the apostles. The word *apostle* means "sent one," and it is as we go into the world with the Gospel that we truly reflect the continuity of our life with the apostles' faith and witness. Merely to regard the succession as an adherence to the apostle's doctrine is not enough. Nor can continuity with the apostles through the laying on of hands fulfill the intent of the matter. The succession is in the way the teachings of the apostles are carried into the world through our lives. Only this practical reproduction of the apostolic witness can, by the grace of God, keep the church from extinction.

20. Elton Trueblood, *The Company of the Committed* (New York: Harper and Row, 1961), 72.

21. Harold Hinton, author of *Fanshen*, and expert on China, expressed this opinion in 1950. He felt that the Chinese church was on its way to extinction. See Leslie Lyall, *God Reigns in China* (London: Hodder and Stoughton, 1985), 178. Religious expediency was especially characteristic of those liberal Christians who had accepted the socialistic teachings of the ecumenical movement, and they generally welcomed the Communist takeover. Ibid., 106.

22. Ibid., 152.

23. Ibid., 157.

24. Ibid.

25. Ibid., 214, 215.

26. Thousands of Chinese churches have been reopened, along with a number of Christian training schools. Most of the imprisoned pastors have been released and have resumed their ministerial duties. These approved functions are under the state-controlled Three Self Patriotic Movement (TSPM; self-governing, self-supporting, and self-propagating) and its sister organization, the China Christian Council.

Most of those worshiping in these reopened congregations are devout Christians, as are their pastors, though there is considerable question about those in the church hierarchy who have collaborated with the Communist government. Because of the identification of the reopened churches with the TSPM and the repressive measures taken by the TSPM against "house churches" that will not join it, most Christians in China—up to 80 percent—remain apart from the TSPM. For a competent review of the present situation, see ibid., 180-222; also Carl Lawrence, *The Church in China* (Minneapolis: Bethany House, 1985), 97-112, 155-56; David H. Adeney, *China: The Church's Long March* (Ventura, Cal.: Regal Books, 1985); cf. G. Thompson Brown, *Christianity in the People's Republic of China* (Atlanta: John Knox Press, 1986), 137-230.

Five

Renewed and
Reaching Out

A PRACTICAL QUESTION NOW NEEDS TO BE RAISED. HOW do we become involved in the ministry of the church? The usual pattern is to think in terms of looking after the church property, working in the altar guild, helping with the every-member canvass, or doing some other little chore around the church. No one will deny that these things need to be done. But is this all that our life of service involves?

"Has Anyone Been Saved Here Lately?"

We must begin by asking once again: What is our mission as the church? The answer lies in recognizing that we are the body of Christ. Therefore, we should be doing what He did on earth. World evangelism, thus, should be the mission, the controlling purpose of the Church, for it was our Lord's controlling purpose—the only reason that the eternal Son threw off the robes of glory and took upon Himself the form of our flesh. He came "to seek and to save that which was lost" (Luke 19:10)—"not to be ministered unto, but to minister, and to give his life a ransom for many" (Matthew 20:28).

An elderly lady in a party of tourists visiting Westminster Abbey focused this issue exactly. She turned to the guide and said, "Young man! Young man! Will you stop your chatter for a moment and tell me—has anyone been saved here lately?"[1]

A strange silence came over the astonished and perhaps embarrassed tour group. Saved in Westminster Abbey? But why not? Isn't that the business of the Church? A church discovering the thrill of revival will know this and will be actively seeking to win the lost. Revival and evangelism, though different in nature, issue from the same source and flow together. A church that does not go out into the world to press the claims of the kingdom would not know revival if it came.

Evangelism might be called the spiritual thermometer of the church. When the body of believers is sick, the evangelistic program is usually the first thing to stagger. Custom and pride will keep other programs going long after their purpose is lost. Yet any church activity that is not expressing the Savior's love for lost men is simply out of touch with the Gospel. How tragic it is when the concern for fellowship, civic improvement, intellectual attainment, social welfare, or some other secondary consideration becomes the controlling passion of church life.

This confusion of priorities is doubtless one of the most bewildering problems confronting the Christian community. The harsh truth is that whenever evangelism is relegated to an incidental place in a church's program, the church begins to die. And unless something happens to reverse the trend, that church will eventually become extinct. The church can continue only as the people of God reproduce their life in each succeeding generation.[2]

This does not happen by accident. We must aim at the target to hit it. The sentimental idea that somehow evangelism will take care of itself, provided we live a good life, has a subtle way of beguiling us to sleep. On the other hand, a constant whirl of activity in the church is no assurance that people are being converted. Crowds may come to the Sunday services, large building programs may be completed, big budgets may be raised, tremendous energy may be expended in many worthwhile things—and evangelism may still be missing. Making Christ known and loved must become a total life commitment.[3]

Winsome Witnesses

Evangelism is ultimately a personal responsibility. No amount of programmed activity in official church meetings can take the place of the day-by-day vocation of personal evangelism. To assume that the formal church organization can operate on one level while the members of the body live differently is wishful thinking. The ministry of the congregation is only a reflection of the lives of individuals in the church, and this is nowhere more apparent than in evangelism.

It is imperative that each of us makes the routine contacts with other people a winsome witness for Christ. Opportunities for lifting up Christ come every day in the normal associations at home, school, and work. We must learn to speak a word for our Savior in the right way and at the right time. Of course, this sensitivity comes through the Holy Spirit and cannot be engineered by human ingenuity. But we *can* find ways to cultivate winsomeness in our personal evangelism. One doesn't have to be obnoxious to be an honest witness.

Winsomeness involves taking a genuine interest in people, listening to them, learning about their problems, showing them by our deeds that we care. When confidence has been gained, then we can explain how the Gospel that has changed our lives can also change theirs.[4]

The church might help develop these traits by providing training classes in soul-winning. This instruction should include basic knowledge of the plan of salvation, supported by key Scripture verses. Every Christian needs to be able to give an unequivocal answer to anyone who wants to know the way to God.

These formal presentations will help communicate what evangelism is all about. But a personal, living example will do much better. The learning disciples need to be brought into close association with those who are already able to demonstrate, by their lives, just how it is done. The church might assist in this by arranging for novices to team up with those more experienced in witnessing.[5] This throws a heavy burden upon the few in the church who are equipped to teach, but there is no other way to do it effectively.

Winsome Programs, Too!

What is stimulated in individual members of the congregation also needs to become part of the official program of the church.[6] Soul-winning and disciple-making should be so fused with the structure of congregational life that if the structure functions at all, evangelism is inevitable.

The church begins by knowing where the people are. Every non-Christian in the area the church serves is a special responsibility. We should locate these people, learn their names, know their family relationships, their social and economic needs—and this information should be followed up with specific prayer and personal concern.[7] These people are more than "prospects"—they are immortal souls, each one of more value in God's sight than all the wealth of the world.

Perhaps specific members of the church could be assigned particular non-Christian families to cultivate. These families could be invited to neighborhood witness activities or home Bible studies.[8] A vigorous visitation effort also needs to be pursued so that every one of these persons is lovingly confronted with the claims of Christ.[9]

This compassion for the lost should be reflected in the worship services of the church. Not every service should be designed in the format of an evangelistic campaign, but the spirit of Christian love should be so apparent as to make any non-Christian in attendance aware of the ever-present invitation to seek God. At times, of course, the whole order of worship can be directed toward the outsider, leading up to a call for decision.

Some churches design all their weekend services with the seekers in mind, though the invitation to receive Christ usually is more subdued.[10] The Sunday school also offers a great opportunity for evangelism. For many children and youth, Sunday school is their only contact with the Gospel, and unless they are won here, they probably will not be reached at all.[11] Teachers should be prepared to deal personally with the issues of salvation both in and outside the classroom.

Likewise, evangelism must be geared into the church's auxiliary organizations, such as the youth fellowship, various women's and men's activities, and the scout troops. These groups often attract people who are not reached through the regular meetings of the church, so any comprehensive program of soul-winning must include them. If these auxiliary organizations are not contributing to the redemptive mission of Christ, why have them in the church?

A Continuous Work

Whatever you do, do not stop. There is no discharge in this warfare. The powers of darkness are always seeking to destroy the souls of men and women. To do battle with the enemy only during special seasons of the year or merely when you feel like it is to abandon the world to the devil the rest of the time. If the Church is to be victorious, we must take the field with the Gospel and maintain the offensive.[12]

The Gospel is always good news. So long as God is pleased to speak to dying men, the story must be told. The moment the Gospel ceases to be heard, the Church ceases to be relevant to the world.

Hence, in witness to her mission, the Church should be winning souls "in season and out of season." The popular practice of going all-out for evangelism in some kind of annual or semiannual event is to be commended to every congregation, but this in itself is not adequate. Sometimes, in fact, these special campaigns merely soothe the consciences of people who prefer to get a year's work of witnessing over in a few days.

There are, of course, advantages in making special efforts to present the Gospel during certain times of the year. But these programs should only intensify an ongoing emphasis. There are multitudes of people who are not reached at all during these special seasons of concern. Many of them might be won if churches would practice a vigil for souls the year round.

By All Means

This ongoing need for outreach underscores the necessity for a variable approach. Any method that God is pleased to use in the salvation of a soul is a good method for that person. Yet each person is different, and what impresses one individual may not have any appeal to another. We must be discerning of the particular need and find appropriate methods of evangelism.

Jesus demonstrated this principle in His ministry. Practically every legitimate method of evangelism used today can be seen in some way in the work of the Master—mass meetings, small groups, healing services, visitation campaigns, personal counseling. He could adjust His method to any situation. The Apostle Paul caught this spirit when he said, "I am made all things to all men, that I might by all means save some" (1 Corinthians 9:22).

Of course, a church should utilize to the fullest its present methods. The need to gear the customary programs of the church to evangelism has already been mentioned. If these activities are meeting the need, there is no reason to change. In this connection, it might be helpful to evaluate your own church's various programs in the light of their effectiveness in reaching your community with the Gospel.

When it is apparent that old methods are not getting the desired results, look around for better ways of doing it. We can learn from our fellow Christians in other churches. There are also many interdenominational organizations that might lift our horizons in certain areas of evangelism. When it comes to ways of communicating the Gospel, no one has a corner on the market.

Yet, sad to say, almost all of us have a tendency to get so obsessed with the two or three methods that have been particularly effective in our experience that we fail to see other, and perhaps more promising, ways of achieving our goal. Some churches act as if their survival were dependent upon a certain technique of evangelism.

While we can appreciate this nostalgia for those methods that brought us to Christ, still we must remain open to new ways the Spirit may have in reaching our generation. Of course, there is no virtue in mere newness. Something new may not be any better. Closer scrutiny will reveal that the new approaches have their limitations too. The point is that we should seek to find the best means of getting the work done. Whether or not the course of action is endorsed by long custom is entirely beside the point. The question is: Will it work?

The Venturing Spirit

It is not my purpose here to go into the myriad of things a church can do. My purpose is simply to point out the need to be imaginative and creative in finding ways to fulfill its mission. There should always be an air of freshness about our approach to the hearts of men.

Do you see a place in your church where the excitement of evangelism is missing? Is it in your Sunday school? Then have you considered revising your curriculum or starting a new class designed to reach a neglected segment of your community? What about deploying your people experienced in small groups to open their homes for an activity with their friends?

Are things bogged down in the youth division? If so, have you thought of organizing a youth witnessing team or sponsoring a contemporary Christian music concert?

What about your men's group? Do they have a vibrant ministry beyond themselves? Is the thrill of personal witnessing evident in visitation programs? Do they ever go out and conduct open-air meetings on the street?[13]

What are your young couples doing to win their friends? If they want to, but don't know how, why not talk it over next Sunday? Perhaps you could try a bowling league as a point of contact. Or full-time homemakers might take to the idea of an afternoon tea in various homes.

What are you doing to harness the media for your evangelistic task? Have you thought about going on radio or TV? Could you operate a telephone service for people in distress? Does your church have a vital program of literature evangelism?[14]

Are you reaping a spiritual harvest through an effective healing ministry in the church?[15] If not, why not? Are there no people around who need such help? The same could be said for the multiple social needs in your community, all of which offer opportunities to present the Gospel at the point where people live.[16]

And what are you doing to share God's love with the unreached peoples in distant lands? How about getting together a team of your members to go overseas next summer to help plant a new church? Do you keep Christ's mandate of world missions continually focused in all your local programs?

Whatever the method, the purpose is to bring your outreach into the mainstream of life. Methods are only effective as they get us involved with people. Where the ministry of Christ is brought to bear upon the felt needs of men and women—body, mind, and soul—and the approach is related to the patterns of life of those we seek to reach, there will always be interest in what we have to say.

Some exciting things are happening today as churches seek greater relevance in the world around them. Some groups are invading the public beaches to give their witness for Christ, using such means as debates, parties, films, and public rallies to set up situations for personal confrontation. Some are moving into high-rise apartment complexes to make their homes points of contact for gospel dialogue. Some are using breakfasts and luncheons to get together professional people for fellowship, prayer, and study of the Word. Some are going deep into gambling dens and red-light districts to start street missions and counseling services. Some Christian athletes are using their popularity to reach young people in football clinics, concluding with an evangelistic rally in a high school auditorium. Some are using youth rehabilitation programs and Christian camps to reach inner-city young people.

The list could go on and on. There is no end to what can be done to introduce people to the Savior. As to what methods are best in your situation, who can say? But whatever is done, whether it be something new or old, methodology has to be incarnated in persons fully available to Jesus Christ.

The Pastor Sets the Pace

Those in leadership roles in the church need to set the pace for others to follow. The pastor especially is positioned to help the people find their place of service. This gifted teacher is not called to do all the work of the church, but to "equip" the congregation for the work of ministry—a work they all share together.[17]

In this capacity the pastor might be compared to a playing coach, whose duty is to prepare the team for the game. The coach knows the players, their abilities, their weaknesses, and he seeks through disciplined nurture to develop the full potential of each person. But as a playing coach, he is not a mere strategist. He plays beside his men, directing the contest from the field, not the bench. "The mark of [the pastor's] success is not the amount of attention which he can focus upon himself, but the redemptive character which emerges in the entire congregation or team."[18]

Nowhere is this more important than in demonstrating the relevance of the Great Commission, not as a special call or a spiritual gift, but as the lifestyle of all Christians. When this idea catches hold in the congregation and each member begins to disciple others, the priesthood of all believers takes form in daily servanthood.

In the final analysis, the ministry of Christ that we share

is not a job; it is a life—the life of God incarnate in the flesh of His Son and now lived by His Spirit in the body of His Church. When this life is harnessed with the yoke of the Master, the Church as a whole becomes a mighty instrument of blessing.

Here is precisely where revival and evangelism become one—the point where love begins to be expressed in action. Where such love abounds, ways will always be found to proclaim the Gospel.

Study Assignments 5

Personal Study

1. Look again at Luke 24:48-49 and Acts 1:8. Why do you think that the outpouring of the Holy Spirit is linked with witnessing?

2. This raises the question: What is meant by evangelism? Is it merely a spoken testimony, or does it involve the presentation of Christ through the total witness of our lives? Write out a definition of evangelism as you understand it.

3. With your definition in mind, paraphrase Acts 1:8.

4. You have already considered how this commission was carried out in Jerusalem and the environs of Judea (Acts 2–7). Now note how the witness of Christ penetrated to regions beyond. Read the account of the revival at Samaria in Acts 8:1-25. Who first carried the Gospel to Samaria, and what served to get him there? Acts 8:1-4.

How did Philip minister in word and deed? Acts 8:5-7.

What effect did his ministry have upon the Samaritans? Acts 8:8-13.

Why did the apostles send Peter and John to Samaria?

5. Read carefully the account of Philip leading the Ethiopian to Christ in Acts 8:28-40. List at least four basic principles of personal evangelism you see in this story.

6. Acts 10:1 through 11:18 tells how the Gospel came to the Gentile house of Cornelius. Why do you suppose that the breakthrough of the Gospel to the non-Jewish world began with a little group of devout people already seeking God? Note Acts 10:1-5, 30-33.

7. From here follow the outreach of the Gospel into the Gentile world in Acts 11:19-30 and 13:1-4. Again, who were the ministers of Christ bearing the Good News to these places?

How did the Jerusalem church help encourage and give direction to this new advance?

How did the Antioch church respond to the physical needs of their brethren in Judea?

When this growing church at Antioch realized the missionary call of the Spirit, how did they react? Acts 13:1-4 (14:25-28; 15:30-35; 18:22-23).

Why do you think this church sensed so keenly their evangelistic responsibility to the world? Sum up your thoughts in a sentence or two.

8. Looking at your church, how is your spiritual life finding expression in your evangelistic work at home and abroad? To help focus the matter, perhaps it would be well to make a mental note of the number of people in your community who have been won to Christ through your witness this past year. In terms of your world vision, how many have gone to the mission field from your church, and how many missionaries do you now fully support? And what about the social needs

of your community? Are you truly involved in healing the heartbreak of those around you?

Group Discussion

In your group this week, come to grips with the work of the Holy Spirit in evangelism. Let each person share his or her view in this respect. Then discuss what you are doing about it. List all the various ways that your church now is seeking to reach the lost. What are your most effective methods? Where is improvement needed? In the light of question 8, are you satisfied? Here is a good place to center your prayers.

NOTES

1. Told by Peter Emmons, *Pattern of Things to Come*, ed. D. McConnell (New York: Friendship Press, 1954), 4.

2. Evangelism was surely on Jesus' mind when He said that nothing could permanently prevail against His Church (Matthew 16:18). This promise followed Peter's strong affirmation of faith in Christ as the Son of the living God (Matthew 16:16; cf. Mark 8:29; Luke 9:20). In essence Jesus said that nothing could keep His church from reproducing as long as the name of Christ is faithfully proclaimed. The rock upon which Jesus said that He would build His church may have had immediate reference to Peter's character or profession of faith, either as an individual or as a representative of all believers; but it was the *expression* of this faith that caused Jesus to see His church as unconquerable. So also today it is the proclamation of Jesus Christ as Lord and Savior that assures the continuation of the apostolic witness.

3. An attempt to define evangelism in its life context and scriptural urgency is my book, *The Heartbeat of Evangelism* (Colorado Springs: NavPress, 1985). For a comprehensive treatment of evangelism, consult the papers and responses of the International Congress on World Evangelization in Lausanne, Switzerland, *Let the Earth Hear His Voice*, ed. J. D. Douglas (Minneapolis: World Wide Publications, 1975). The volumes containing the wide-ranging addresses and seminars at the two International Conferences for Itinerant Evangelists in Amsterdam, Netherlands, also offer timely direction by leading evangelicals. Both

are edited by J. D. Douglas and published by World Wide Publications: *The Work of an Evangelist* (1984) and *The Calling of an Evangelist* (1987).

4. What can and cannot be done in effective personal evangelism is painfully evident in the little book by Joseph Bayly, *The Gospel Blimp* (Grand Rapids: Zondervan, 1966). It is a walloping satire on artificial evangelism.

As to winning souls without being repulsively professional, each person will have to let the Holy Spirit teach him or her the most natural way in each situation. Many books offer helpful guidance, such as Paul E. Little, *How to Give Away Your Faith* (Downers Grove, Ill.: InterVarsity Press, 1966); Bill Bright, *Witnessing Without Fear* (San Bernardino: Here's Life Publishers, 1987); Joseph C. Aldrich, *Life-style Evangelism* (Portland: Multnomah Press, 1978); Rebecca Manley Pippert, *Out of the Saltshaker* (Downers Grove, Ill.: InterVarsity Press, 1979); Mark McCloskey, *Tell It Often–Tell It Well* (San Bernardino: Here's Life Publishers, 1986); W. Oscar Thompson, Jr., *Concentric Circles of Concern* (Nashville: Broadman Press, 1981); and Leighton Ford, *The Power of Story: Rediscovering the Oldest, Most Natural Way to Reach People for Christ* (Colorado Springs: NavPress, 1994).

5. An excellent example of this kind of training is the program developed by the Reverend James Kennedy at the Coral Ridge Presbyterian Church in Fort Lauderdale, Florida. In this church each person trained in personal evangelism is expected to train two more who in turn can train others. The program involves weekly classes at the church in conjunction with on-the-job training in home visitation evangelism. Needless to say, the church has experienced phenomenal growth. Information about the training program may be obtained from Evangelism Explosion, Box 23820, Ft. Lauderdale, Florida, 33307. The basic method of this program is contained in the training manual by James Kennedy, *Evangelism Explosion*, 3d ed. (Wheaton, Ill.: Tyndale House, 1983).

6. As with personal evangelism, there are many instruction materials that explain how evangelism can be brought into the various programs of the church. Most denominations will be glad to supply such information. In addition to the official publications of your church, the following books are recommended: Lewis A. Drummond, *Leading Your Church in Evangelism* (Nashville: Broadman Press, 1975); Win and Charles Arn, *The Master's Plan for Making Disciples* (Pasadena: Church Growth, 1982); *A Guide to Evangelism*, ed. Clive Calver et al. (Basingstoke, Hants, UK: Marshall, Morgan and Scott, 1984); and Carl F. George, *Prepare Your Church for the Future* (Tarrytown, N.Y.: Revell, 1991). As to trends in the future affecting the church, one of the best treatments is Leith Andersen's *Dying for Change* (Minneapolis: Bethany House, 1990).

For further practical help in evangelism, see the four-volume reproducible notebook containing the presentations at the American Festival of Evangelism in Kansas City, 1981. (Write to American Festival of Evangelism, P. O. Box 17093, Washington, D.C. 20041.) This publication includes contributions by some two hundred church leaders. Another series with a representative group of evangelism leaders, both Protestant and Roman Catholic, is edited by Glenn C. Smith. The first of the four volumes is *Evangelizing Adults*, jointly published by

Tyndale House in Wheaton, Ill., and the Paulist National Catholic Evangelization Association, Washington, D.C., 1985.

The profuse church growth literature also gives insight. *Church Growth: State of the Art*, ed. C. Peter Wagner with Win Arn and Elmer Towns (Wheaton, Ill.: Tyndale House, 1986), is a summation of the movement. A good introduction also is Kent R. Hunter's book, *Foundations for Church Growth* (Corunna, Ind.: Church Growth Center, 1994). For a view of some different models of church growth, check Elmer Towns, John Vaughan, and David J. Seifert, *The Complete Book of Church Growth*, 2d ed. (Wheaton, Ill.: Tyndale House, 1982); and Elmer Towns, *10 of Today's Most Innovative Churches* (Ventura, Cal.: Regal, 1990).

7. The books cited in reference to church evangelism and visitation work will give practical help in how prospects can be found. Charles S. Mueller discusses the importance of learning the geographical area of primary concern to a church and understanding community social groups in *The Strategy of Evangelism* (St. Louis: Concordia, 1965).

8. Most of the principles discussed in reference to small groups will apply here, except that the atmosphere of a purely friendship group is more social and recreational in the beginning. In addition to the sources cited already, you might see Richard Peace, *Small Group Evangelism* (Downers Grove, Ill.: InterVarsity Press, 1985); Ralph Neighbor, *Target Group Evangelism* (Nashville: Broadman Press, 1975); Dale E. Galloway, *20/20 Vision: How to Create a Successful Church* (Portland, Ore.: Scott Publishing Co., 1986); and Bob and Betty Jacks with Ron Wormser, Sr., *Your Home, a Lighthouse* (San Bernardino: Churches Alive, 1986).

9. There is no lack of information on the organization and method of visitation evangelism. Check with the appropriate office of your denomination. Each local church will need to use the approach most suited to its situation. For some good ideas, in addition to the Evangelism Explosion program already noted, read Roy J. Fish's *Every Member Evangelism for Today* (New York: Harper and Row, 1976), an update of J. E. Connant's classic *Every Member Evangelism*, and Jack Hyles's *Let's Build an Evangelistic Church* (Murfreesboro: Sword of the Lord, 1962).

10. The Willow Creek Community Church outside Chicago under the leadership of Bill Hybels has premiered this concept of ministry. In the space of twenty years the church has become one of the largest congregations in America. A good explanation of this approach to evangelism and its methodology is the *Willow Creek Community Church Leaders Handbook*, 2nd ed., prepared by David L. Olsson (Barrington, Ill: Willow Creek Association, 1993). How this church views its audience is discussed by Lee Strobel, *Inside the Mind of Unchurched Harry and Mary* (Grand Rapids: Zondervan, 1993). To feel the heartbeat of the church and its sense of mission, read *Becoming a Contagious Christian* by Bill Hybels and Mark Mettleberg (Grand Rapids: Zondervan, 1994).

11. There are many ways that a Sunday school can implement evangelistic programs. If you are wondering what can be done, ask your denominational headquarters to supply you with information, or consult some of the many guide books that deal with this subject, such as Edwin J. Potts, *Evangelism in the Sunday School* (Chicago: National Sunday School Association, 1960); E. P. Barrett, *A*

Guide for Sunday School Evangelism (Wheaton, Ill.: Evangelical Teacher Training Association, 1956); and Mary Latham, Teacher: You Are an Evangelist (Kansas City: Beacon Hill, 1963).

12. An interesting summary of "warfare strategy" is the little book by James I. Wilson, The Principles of War (Annapolis, Md.: Christian Books in Annapolis, 1964). The author, an army officer, shows that following certain principles of warfare always tends toward success in battle, but neglecting or ignoring these principles inevitably tends toward defeat. To bring this into the contemporary discussion of spiritual warfare, especially emphasizing prayer, check John Dawson, Taking Our Cities for God (Altamonte Springs, Fla.: Creation House, 1989) and Ed Murphy, Handbook for Spiritual Warfare (Nashville: Nelson Communications, 1992).

13. One of the most helpful discussions of this approach is the manual for Salvation Army workers by Lyell Rader, Rediscovering the Open Air Meeting (New York: The Salvation Army Supply, 1966).

14. A good statement in this regard is George Verwer's book Literature Evangelism (Chicago: Moody Press, 1963); also E. Henry Edwards and Faris D. Whitesell, Sowing Gospel Seed (Chicago: Moody Press, 1954).

15. The healing of the body is vitally related to the healing of the soul. A church that ignores the ministry of healing not only misses a great opportunity to serve human need, but also fails to realize its evangelistic potential. If some reading in this field is desired, see S. I. McMillen, None of These Diseases (Westwood, N.J.: Fleming H. Revell, 1963); Paul Tournier, The Healing of Persons (New York: Harper and Row, 1965); John Wimber's Power Evangelism (1986) and Power Healing (1987), published by Harper and Row; and Living Free in Christ, a book on inner healing by Neal T. Anderson (Ventura, Cal.: Regal, 1993).

16. What can be done is discussed by Richard Stoll Armstrong in Service Evangelism (Philadelphia: Westminster Press, 1979) and Harvie M. Conn, Evangelism: Doing Justice and Preaching Grace (Grand Rapids: Zondervan, 1982).

17. For a brief discussion of the equipping ministry of the pastor, see my note on Ephesians 4:11-12 in The Master Plan of Evangelism, 34. An excellent amplification of this passage and its implications for the church is in Fish, Every Member, 14-18. For a full treatment of the subject, read Bill Hull's The Pastor as Disciplemaker (Old Tappan, N.J.: Fleming H. Revell, 1988).

18. Trueblood, The Incendiary Fellowship, 44.

Six

Planning a Revival Meeting

WE MUST NOW CONSIDER THE PLANNING OF CHURCH revival meetings, by whatever name they may be called. You may wonder why we have taken so long to introduce this subject. But the reason has already been implied. It is necessary to see these special services within the context of the total church mission and strategy. If revivals are isolated from the ongoing program of the church, as if we can have revival only at particular times or through certain methods, then we have missed the whole meaning of revival. Obviously a series of revival meetings is not enough. Still, where the services bring into focus the meaning of vital Christian experience and create a situation for people to seek God in earnest, there is no reason why a revival meeting cannot live up to its name.

Keep the Purpose Clear

Remember that our first concern in a revival meeting is to awaken the church to her potential power. "Judgment must begin at the house of God. . . ." (1 Peter 4:17), which is another way of saying that the saints must move up if the sinners are to move in. There is no place for superficiality in program or message. If the revival is to reach far, it must go deep.

Implementing this concern will mean that the great holiness themes of Scripture will need to be stressed in the meetings. Simple Bible exposition is the need, with an emphasis upon daily living of the victorious Christian faith. We must get down to the practical disciplines of life, giving attention to such needs as daily worship, family religion, personal ethics, social obligations, witnessing in our work, and world missions.

Of course, the evangelistic challenge to the outsider cannot be neglected. Unbelievers brought into the meetings should understand what they must do to be saved; and they should be given opportunity to express their need. But the primary burden of a revival meeting is to get the church to be the church. A church revival then becomes a launching pad for all-out evangelism.

Preparation Is the Key

Revival meetings may come about in many ways. In some cases they are a traditional part of the annual church calendar. In other instances they may be scheduled in cooperation with a larger district or conference program. Sometimes a congregation just decides to have a revival meeting because the time seems right.

In any event, a revival meeting, like any other effective church program, is going to require the full exercise of every talent and gift bestowed by God. It involves painstaking planning. God may very well overrule our plans and send revival in a way we have not expected—an option always welcome when God chooses to exercise it.[1] Even so, this possibility does not excuse us from doing everything we can to prepare the way of the Lord. What happens during the meeting usually reflects the vision and dedication that has gone into it. In fact, most of the real work is done before the formal meetings begin.

This need for preparation underscores again the fact that the church must have a nucleus of disciples willing to let God have His way in their lives. As this group gives leadership to others, and more become involved in the ministry of the church, a strong working force for revival is assured. These people, strategically placed in positions of influence, put the needed "get up and go" into the effort.

Gear to Your Situation

Local conditions will determine the particular structure of the revival meeting. Since every situation is different, adjustments will have to be made in any scheme proposed by this or any other book.[2] Common sense is probably the best policy.

Look at the situation from every angle. What kinds of revival meetings have been tried in the past? How have they succeeded? Weigh carefully the working schedules of your people, their patterns of leisure, their attitudes toward various methods of evangelism. What type of program would appeal most to their interests? When is the best time to have a meeting? How long should it last? Where would be the best place to conduct services? Will special workers be invited to assist in the effort?[3] How can the revival emphasis be extended into the community? What will be a realistic budget, and how will the funds be raised? What will be done to follow up those who respond at the meetings? How does the church plan to continue the revival concern? These and other questions should be considered objectively in the early stages of planning.

Special Focus Needed?

Most meetings will follow a general spiritual life and evangelistic theme. However, sometimes you may want to give the message a special focus. For example, it might center on prayer, witnessing, or Bible prophecy. Possibly the services could follow the pattern of a youth crusade, family life seminar, mission conference,[4] Sunday school revival,[5] or lay-witness mission.[6]

A well-balanced program should include various ministries of outreach during the day. There might be early prayer services, groups meeting at breakfast or lunch, morning study periods, afternoon visitation or training sessions, evening youth groups, and any number of other activities scheduled to supplement the featured night rallies.[7] On rare occasions you might even want to arrange a "nonstop" series of services in the church for a given period of time.[8]

The church building may be the focal point of activity, but do not restrict services to this central meeting place.

Something should be done to get the revival out to where people live. Meetings of various kinds can be arranged in homes, schools, factories, businesses, hotels, restaurants, jails, hospitals, theaters, and on the streets. Mass communications can be used to carry the revival message still farther out into the community.

Leave no stone unturned in working out the details of your plan. Be imaginative! During the time of scheduled meetings an effort should be made literally to saturate the area with the witness of revival. The more different ways people can be involved in the effort, the better it will be. The only limitation to what can be done is the personnel you have available to direct the program.

Set the Schedule

Once the general guidelines for the revival meeting have been determined, dates need to be set and the church calendar cleared of any competing programs. It would be well also to check with other community activities to avoid conflicts of interest as far as possible. Where special workers are to be invited to assist in the meetings, it may be necessary to make arrangements long in advance.

The actual organizing of a meeting should begin to take shape about four months prior to the event. By this time committees should begin to function. Three months before the scheduled meetings, things should be well under way, with the pace accelerating as the time of the meetings draws near.

Delegate Authority

Thorough preparation necessarily requires organization. No amount of spiritual dedication is a substitute for this tedious work. To leave the preparation of a revival meeting to impulse is to discredit the intelligence God has given to His people. Organization alone is no sign of Christian commitment, but on the other hand, God is not the author of confusion.

The official responsibility for planning the meeting usually rests with a commission answerable to the church board. This group normally is composed of representatives from every department of the church. The pastor, as a member of the group, naturally will have a lot to say about any revival plans, but responsibility for setting up and directing the meeting rests with the whole body. Sometimes these committees of the church may seem cumbersome and unnecessarily slow, but if we are to expect total church participation in the effort, we will have to work through the established channels.

The revival commission should communicate to each member of the congregation exactly what he or she will be expected to do as part of the revival. Everyone should be enlisted in the effort in some way. Work responsibilities must be spelled out in detail and then assigned to specific people.

Usually these areas of responsibility are delegated to committees of one or more persons, depending upon the size of the church. Where existing committees already have jurisdiction in a given area, such as visitation or music, work in that area can be given to them. In areas where the church has no group presently working, special committees can be set up. The precise structure of these working groups is not important. All that matters is that they be able to handle the work assigned to them and that they are willing to do it.

Working Out the Details

The following areas of responsibility embrace the general setup for a local church meeting. Not everything suggested in every category can be carried out in a revival effort, but something in each area should be done. As you go through these areas, note what applies in your case.

(1) *Prayer*. Revival comes through prayer. To overlook this in planning a meeting would be tragic indeed. So in addition to intensifying the regular intercessory ministry of the church, it would be well to undergird the revival with some special programs of prayer.[9] Prayer meetings can be scheduled in various homes and businesses preceding and continuing through the meeting.[10] Prayer times can also be arranged around breakfasts and luncheons in hotels and restaurants. Taking an idea from Pentecost, prayer services might be scheduled for the ten days before the meeting—or perhaps a twenty-four hour prayer vigil just before the revival. Pre-service prayer meetings can be announced. The congregation could be asked to pause for a moment of prayer at a given time each day. Prayer lists can be circulated to shut-ins. Reminders to pray can be placed in hymnals, near telephones, and in all church mailings. Prayer requests can be sent to other churches. To help sharpen the spiritual vision for revival, a prayer retreat might be scheduled for all committee chairmen and church leaders. A dedication service for all the revival workers could be held the day before the formal meeting starts.

(2) *Prospects.* The church should always have an up-to-date list of people for whom particular prayer is being offered and continuous concern manifested. If this is not the case in your church, something will have to be done about it, to focus the outreach of the revival.

(3) *Visitation.* We must "go after" people if we want to win them. This continuing responsibility of the church should be strengthened by the revival. Some visitation calls may be simply for the purpose of making friends and inviting them to the revival meetings. More experienced callers can visit targeted people with the idea of presenting the claims of Christ and asking for a decision. These assignments are made from the prospect list. Usually the visitation callers meet in the evening for briefing and prayer, perhaps following a light meal. They are paired in teams and sent out to call on assigned homes. After the calls are completed, they return and report the results. If this is not already a part of the church program, it certainly needs to be instituted for the revival. As part of the visitation, interviews might be arranged for the evangelist and pastor to visit with city officials and leading public figures.

(4) *Lay witness.* There is no revival in the church without the joyous witness of ordinary Christians; nor is there anything more convincing to the skeptical world. Such witness should be encouraged in the public services and in small group settings as well. Those groups already meeting can enlarge their outreach by inviting new friends in for fellowship and Bible study. New groups could be started to address the interests of particular professions such as doctors, school teachers, or foreign students. Afternoon teas could feature dynamic women telling about their Christian experience.

Following the services each night, people could be invited to various homes for "after-glow" discussions. If help is needed to maintain so many concurrent outreaches, laymen from other churches in your denomination would probably be glad to come in and share their witness.

(5) *Sunday school.* Since this is the greatest agency for evangelism, it would be virtually impossible to have much of a revival without bringing the Sunday school into it. Enlist every teacher in the effort. Classes can assist in promoting attendance. Perhaps the revival meeting could coincide with a record attendance drive[11] or "decision day"[12] emphasis in the Sunday school.

(6) *Children.* Something special should be done to make children aware of their place in the kingdom. Perhaps children's services could be arranged in the afternoon or preceding the evening rally. It might be possible to announce the meetings through the grade school. Of course, good leadership is essential, and you may need to secure a gifted children's worker from outside your own church.

(7) *Youth.* Here is where the action usually starts. Young people want to be challenged, and when you get their attention, revival makes sense. Seek the cooperation of the high school teachers and coaches. Get names of all students and send them a personal letter inviting them to the revival meeting. Contact all youth organizations in the community such as the Boy Scouts, Girl Scouts, 4-H Clubs, and Hi Y. Extend to each an invitation to attend the revival services as a group. Work with campus organizations to reach college students. Involve young people in your visitation efforts. Arrange some functions especially for the youth, such as a breakfast each morning or a banquet on Saturday night before the public

service. An open discussion might be arranged for the college set. "Talk-back" sessions after the evening services are also popular with this age group.

(8) *Music.* Revival sets people to singing. To provide direction to this joyful impulse, a great musical program each evening should be arranged. Secure a good song leader. See that a choir is present each night. Existing choirs of the church can be used, or a special group can be formed for the meetings. Trained accompanists will need to be ready. Sometimes a band or orchestra can be assembled. Make sure sufficient song books are available. Select a theme song for the meeting, singing it each night to open or close the services.

(9) *Nursery.* To encourage young couples and single parents to attend, arrange for child care during the meetings. The best way is to have a nursery staffed with competent attendants. If your church does not have such facilities, then a nursery should be set up in a home. You may also compile a list of trustworthy baby-sitters who would be glad to go to the house of young parents and stay with their children for a reasonable fee.

(10) *Attendance.* Though most of the aforementioned areas of responsibility involve attendance, some matters along this line would require special attention. For example, you could promote a "fill-a-pew" plan several nights. This is a system whereby each pew in the church is assigned to a captain who is expected to fill the seats by inviting friends to the services. Another way to stimulate interest is to designate a particular group for recognition each night, such as the official board, women's society, or young couples' class. Probably one of the most productive methods of encouraging atten-

dance is to invite guest delegations to the services. The invitations should be extended personally to every church, civic club, industry, and business in the community. It must be done well in advance, and assurance must be given that seats will be reserved so that each group may sit together as a body. In some places it will be necessary to arrange transportation for those wanting to attend the meetings.

(11) *Publicity.* Let the community know that you plan a revival. Start submitting news stories to local newspapers several months before the meetings. Try to get off of the religious page and into the news section. It would be worthwhile to place an eye-catching ad in the paper on the day the meeting begins and continue a small notice throughout the days of the meetings. Give announcements to all radio and TV stations that report local news. Posters may be put in prominent places around town. Ask your people to place bumper stickers on their cars, and also give them a plentiful supply of cards and leaflets to send to their friends. The young people could distribute throughout the community printed folders describing the meeting. Flyers can be made available to food stores to pack with groceries. A large sign might be put up in front of the church and, if possible, a streamer across the highway. Have some of the ladies use a crisscross telephone directory to call every number within several miles of the church and invite the people to the meetings. Spot announcements can be arranged on local radio and TV stations. Often it is possible, too, to have your visiting workers interviewed on local talk shows and by newspaper reporters.

(12) *Facilities.* The place of public meeting should be arranged for worship. See that the building is clean, hymn-

books neatly arranged, floors swept, and so forth. Also take care of things like lighting, temperature, and ventilation. Make sure well in advance of each night's meeting that the public address system is working. Be ready to provide extra seats and any special equipment needed in the service. Sometimes it may be necessary to make special arrangements for the after-glow service.

(13) *Ushers.* Those who come to the services should be made to feel at home. Greeters stationed at each entrance before and after the services can help create a friendly atmosphere. Of course, a sufficient number of ushers should be present to assist in seating people and receiving the offering. They should also be prepared to handle any disturbances that may occur. Parking attendants may be outside to help direct traffic.

(14) *Hospitality.* A worker is worthy of his hire. Arrangements will need to be made to care for the visiting workers' lodging, food, and possibly transportation. It might also be nice to plan a reception for them some night after the service.

(15) *Finance.* Any well-prepared program today costs money—a lot more than most churches realize. What this will be and how the amount will be raised is something that should be agreed on well in advance.[13] Those responsible for carrying out these policies should prepare a tentative budget, receive and deposit all offerings, solicit special contributions, pay all bills, and submit to the church board an audited report when the meetings are over.

(16) *Follow-up.* The enduring value of the revival is determined largely by the direction given those who make commitments. Members involved in follow-up will usually need

special training. The nature of follow-up work will be discussed in the next chapter.

There Are No Shortcuts

The responsibilities briefly outlined here are basic to any revival meeting. As already emphasized, specific plans and committees will need to be adjusted to the situation of each church, but *something* should be done in each area if the revival is to be truly dynamic.

Where adequate preparation is not made, merely having a series of public meetings is not recommended. Most so-called revival meetings should never be conducted. Rather than stumbling halfheartedly through the forms of another meeting, it would be best to go to work in laying the foundation for a real revival, looking toward full-scale public meetings when the church is ready.

A revival crusade demands sacrifices. It means hard work. It will take time and money. There will be innumerable difficulties to overcome, any one of which could be defeating. To see your plans come true, there must be methodical, painstaking, undaunted determination to have revival at any cost.

Study Assignments 6

Personal Study

1. Read the account of the revival at Ephesus in Acts 18:18–20:1. How did the work get started?

When Apollos came to town and began to preach in the synagogue, what limited the spiritual effectiveness of his ministry?

Apparently the eloquent Apollos received more understanding of the Gospel through the witness of Aquila and Priscilla (Acts 18:26-28), but what effect did his early ministry have upon those who followed his teaching?

When Paul again came to Ephesus and learned about these men who only knew the message of John the Baptist, how did he deal with the problem?

With this little group now awakened by the Spirit, Paul proceeded to gather the spiritually sensitive out of the synagogue (Acts 19:8). When opposition came to his ministry, they withdrew to a private home where Paul continued to instruct the learners in the way of Jesus (19:9). Many miraculous works of charity also were done by Paul (19:11-12). But most significantly, within the next two years all of the inhabitants of that province in Asia heard the Gospel of Christ. How did it happen? Note Acts 19:10 (19:26).

Look for some other evidences of real revival in this church. Note Acts 19:13-20.

2. As you think about the development of this revival—beginning with a dedicated couple, then going to a small band, then to a larger group out of the synagogue, and finally to the multitudes of the area—how does this reflect upon the pattern of revival seen elsewhere?

3. List some of the ways Paul ministered at Ephesus. Note the following references: Acts 18:18; 19:1-2, 5, 8; 20:1, 4.

4. What does Paul's statement in 1 Corinthians 9:22 say about his method of ministry? Put this verse in your own words.

5. In thinking about a revival meeting as one way of reaching people, how do you see this method making a real contribution to your church's continuing outreach ministry?

6. What do you conceive to be the primary goal of this kind of effort? Is it aimed at the church or the world? Explain what you mean.

7. In implementing your objective, how extensive should be the program of such a meeting? With this in mind, note some things that can be done to make the meeting more effective. Be specific.

8. What part in the revival preparation are you willing to assume?

Group Discussion

Your group today should get at the purpose for a revival meeting or, for that matter, any kind of "spiritual-life-emphasis" program. Zero in on your objectives and from this consider your methods. Discuss your experiences in such meetings. Then work out some realistic plans for your situation now. These guidelines for action may give content to your prayers.

NOTES

1. When revival comes to a whole congregation, we need not worry about methodology in a meeting. The Spirit of God will take care of the situation Himself, and any method then will work. But where a church has only a small segment who are in the full sway of the Spirit, as is the case in most situations, utmost care must be exercised in seeking to involve larger numbers in the meeting.

2. In addition to books already cited, helpful counsel in preparing for revival meetings may be found in George Sweeting, The Evangelistic Campaign (Chicago: Moody Press, 1955) and John R. Bisagno, The Power of Positive Evangelism (Nashville: Broadman Press, 1968). Denominational headquarters will have helpful material to assist local congregations, as will various evangelistic organizations. Concerning the larger context of citywide crusades, see Sterling W. Huston, Crusade Evangelism and the Local Church (Minneapolis: World Wide Publications, 1984).

3. God has given some people in the church the special office of evangelist (Ephesians 4:11; Acts 21:8; 2 Timothy 4:5). This does not imply that others are not called to evangelize; it simply emphasizes the particular leadership function of this gifted person in the ministry of the whole body of Christ. The church should avail herself of people who have this obvious ability. However, it would be well to check thoroughly into the previous ministry of such persons before one is called to lead in your situation. Like everything else about the human equation, evangelists have different talents and temperaments, and the church should understand these differences in deciding upon the evangelist most suited to its need. There are times, too, when a pastor or missionary might be the first choice to lead a given meeting. Whatever the choice of leadership, it would be well to keep in mind Billy Graham's A Biblical Standard for Evangelists (Minneapolis: World Wide Publications, 1984), which came out of the International Conferences for Itinerant Evangelists at Amsterdam. Another statement on expectations of evangelists was drawn up at the North American Conference for Itinerant Evangelists in Louisville (1994).

4. Such a conference revolves around Christ's commission to disciple all nations, with missionaries fresh from the field usually leading the services. The program may be concentrated on a weekend or extend for a week or more, culminating in a faith-promise offering and appeal for commitment to mission service. For practical ideas in developing missions conferences, contact your mission board or Advancing Churches in Missions Commitment, P. O. Box ACMC, Wheaton, Illinois 60189.

5. In this kind of meeting the Sunday school meets usually for forty-five minutes before or after the regular preaching service each evening. Where classes meet before the rally, instruction may be given in the subject later to be expounded by the preacher. If classes meet after the rally, they can provide a means for discussing the sermon or having a follow-up Bible study. Usually on the final night there is a dedication service. A teacher-training class could be scheduled during the day.

6. A lay-witness approach centers in personal testimony by dynamic laypersons

who come to share their experiences, usually for a weekend of meetings. The visitors are entertained in the homes of your people, which adds to their witness penetration. Fellowship dinners, prayer breakfasts, discussion groups, personal visitation, and recreational activities can supplement the public meetings.

7. Visiting workers can handle some of these meetings, but the pastor and other church leaders will need to carry their load. The invited evangelist should be consulted ahead of time if he is expected to lead these extra services.

8. Such services usually are scheduled for a period of twelve to twenty-four hours. Preaching periods may be interspersed with singing, testimonies, prayer, discussion groups, films, training classes, debates, and so forth. The idea is to have scheduled activities going on continuously, with people free to come and go as they wish. A prayer vigil can continue the meeting through the night.

9. For very helpful information regarding united prayer initiatives in the local church, see Robert Bakke's work, *The Concert of Prayer: Back to the Future* (Minneapolis: Evangelical Free Church of America, 1993); also the books of Edgardo Silvoso, *That None Should Perish* (Ventura, Cal.: Regal Books, 1994); C. Peter Wagner, *Churches That Pray* (Ventura, Cal.: Regal Books, 1994); and Evelyn Christensen, *A Study Guide for Evangelism Praying* (Colorado Springs: A.D. 2000 International Women's Track, 1994).

10. These informal prayer meetings can be conducted at different locations in the community and at different times during the day and night. The groups may meet every day or only once or twice a week depending upon the situation. Announce the schedule in all church media. Invite people to attend the meetings best suited to their schedule and locality. Each group should have a host and a prayer leader.

The host sees that everything is ready for the meeting and welcomes the people as they arrive. The leader is responsible for conducting the services. Always start and end on time. See that everyone is acquainted. The service may consist of a brief Bible reading, testimonies, sharing of requests, and a general session of prayer in which everyone is invited to participate. Such meetings usually last between forty-five minutes and an hour.

11. An attendance goal is set for the Sunday school and broken down by departments and classes. Teachers are asked to contact every pupil and urge their attendance. On the appointed Sunday, when the roll has been taken in the classes, the Sunday school students go into the church sanctuary. After a few songs, the evangelist is introduced, and his message takes the place of the usual Sunday school lesson. He presents the plan of salvation and gives an invitation. The service may go on into the regular church hour or dismiss in time for morning worship.

12. A "decision day" follows much the same pattern as the "record attendance day," except that it is aimed only at the juniors, intermediates, and youth, and it does not necessarily involve any attendance campaign. However, it should be preceded by the teacher's personal counsel with pupils who are not clear in their experience with Christ. The decision-day approach is not recommended unless this pre-service visit has been completed, preferably in the home.

13. Where special workers are invited to help in the services, financial

obligations should be frankly discussed at the time arrangements are made. Persons engaged full time in this itinerant ministry will be glad to discuss their policy with church leaders. Evangelists and their families usually are supported entirely by the remuneration given to them in these meetings. They deserve a fair compensation for their labors.

Seven

The Importance of Follow-up

R EVIVALS SHOULD NEVER END! SPECIAL CRUSADES have their place as a way of stimulating concern, but the spiritual reality of revival is not dependent upon big meetings to keep it going. So how can the spirit of revival be maintained?

Recognize the Problem

Too often there is a tendency to "let down" after the formal crusade is over. Some of this may be due to emotional exhaustion—a necessary release from the tension that follows a sustained period of concentration. But this post-crusade letdown can also be symptomatic of spiritual decline, calling into question the genuineness of the revival itself.

Naturally, those swept into the revival current merely on the wave of emotional sentimentality will soon fall away.

Since they live more by feeling than by faith, when the enthusiasm of the meeting subsides, they have nothing to hold on to. Such people can be salvaged, but they will need to be brought to a true Christian commitment anchored in the Word of God.

Others may have made a sincere decision to follow Christ but are so immature in their faith that they are easily discouraged and overwhelmed by temptation. When these new Christians are not established in the meaning of their experience, as so often happens, it is easy to understand why they fall away.

But probably even more frustrating to the effect of revival is the way some older Christians fail to bear fruit after the meeting is over. It is not that they cease to identify with the church, but that they lose their zeal to see the revival spread and deepen. After a while they become content to coast along in the same old patterns as before. Mediocrity sets in. Some who were prominent in the meeting become casual in their responsibility to the church. The blessings of the revival are appreciated, and the remembrance of former days may be venerated, but there is no real effort to perpetuate the dedication that called them forth.

Retreat Brings Defeat

What we may fail to comprehend is that the fruits of revival can endure only as the conditions for revival are maintained. There must be continual openness to the Spirit's direction. As He leads on to deeper truths in Christ, we must follow. Where we see a wrong deed or attitude in our life, obedience to Christ demands that we confess our sin, forsake it, and by faith renew our dedication. Moreover, as we grow in grace and knowledge, we should also grow in expressing our faith through deeds of love.

Complacency invariably undermines revival. When the spirit of sacrifice wanes, people become self-conscious, and this disposition leads to criticism and dissension within the church. Minor concerns come to the fore, and before long people get so involved in their own little pursuits that they have no time for soul-winning.

As the Christian community withdraws into itself, the church is pressed to think in terms of self-preservation. Energy is diverted from attack to defense. Daring faith, which before had swept everything in its wake, now becomes halting and conciliatory. Things may go along all right for a while, but the thrill of victory is gone. Revival loses its radiance. It does not die; it just fades away. The life gradually leaks out of it; the vision vanishes. Regrettably, this seems to be the condition of many churches today.[1]

There are those who seek to keep alive something of the revival witness. Unfortunately, these stalwart believers often become withdrawn from the leadership of the church. They are a stabilizing influence and have a very wholesome ministry, but even they may fail to reproduce their life and vision in others.

Follow-Up of New Christians

Thorough follow-up of new believers is the place to begin. The church must provide incentive and leadership to those who have resolved to obey Christ. Without such an effort the revival has no enduring value. We dare not get so thrilled with the rescue of the perishing that we leave those sheep already gathered to become the prey of wolves.

New Christians are especially in need of personal care.[2] They are but "babes" in their new life in Christ (1 Peter 2:2) and, like any infant, must have spiritual guardians to feed, protect, and guide them in order to survive. This can only be done by fellow Christians who have a shepherd's heart. Materials and programs, excellent as they may be, are no substitute for loving, personal attention.

With this in mind, the church will need some kind of system to assure that each new disciple has a Christian friend. This is a matter too crucial to leave to chance. It might be that a special committee should be set up to direct this program.[3] The committee could assign counselors to young converts and receive regular progress reports from the counselors. If a less formal structure is desired, perhaps the follow-up could be supervised by one of the growth groups in the church.

Regardless of the way the program is structured, it will involve a lot of people, and the number needed will increase as the revival harvest grows. Such personal follow-up does not come by wishful thinking. People must be enlisted and trained for this work. Again, the little nucleus of committed Christians around which the revival emerged will be most sensitive to this need, and they will need to lead the way for others.

Immediate Help

Follow-up of new Christians, like any pediatric care, should begin at birth. For this reason, it is well to have trained counselors ready during all public church services to assist those who respond to the invitation. Normally they should be of the same sex and near the same age, except when dealing with children or members of the family. It is customary for the counselor to go forward and take a position next to the seeker or to stand by and wait for assignment by the pastor. If the encounter takes place at an altar, the counselor may want to come to the inside of the communion rail. In an inquiry room, the counselor may sit next to the seeker.

The seeker should be allowed to pray without interruption as long as he or she wants. When it is time to speak, the counselor can initiate an introduction and, by asking questions, help the person to clarify what has happened.[4] The assumption is that the seeker has something to settle either by confirming a decision made earlier or by making a new commitment. The Bible can be used as a reference as needed. If the seeker does not seem satisfied, the counselor will need to find out why and deal with the problem.

When the matter has been resolved, the respondent may be invited to bear witness to his or her faith by offering a prayer of thanksgiving to God. Then counsel may be given regarding basic disciplines of the Christian life.[5] The point of particular emphasis should be obedience to all the revealed will of God. A gospel tract or a simple Bible study guide can help further "nail down" the counsel given.[6]

Before the victorious seeker leaves, it is well to introduce him to others of like mind who will encourage his faith.[7] If someone other than the counselor is to carry on the follow-up, this would be an ideal time to get them together. Such an introduction might also lead to some kind of group association such as a prayer cell or Bible study fellowship.

Continuing Care

Hereafter the young disciple should be contacted regularly by a follow-up worker, preferably once or twice a week for several months. These casual visits need not be long, nor should they appear to be routine. The idea is just to get together as friends and share the things of God.[8]

If it is discovered through these contacts that the person still is not clear in his Christian experience, the problem can be discussed. After all, the person is still seeking reality and is still open for instruction. It would be nice if everyone had all their questions and fears resolved at the time of their conversion, but it doesn't usually work out that way.

Even in the case of those genuinely converted, there will still be hurdles to clear. Where some problem is detected, such as knowing how to deal with doubts and temptations, the follow-up worker can address it sympathetically out of his or her own experience and Bible knowledge. Practical help can also be given in the realm of personal devotions, family worship, social ethics, and witnessing. If the person is pursuing a Bible study program, the worker can also use these times to good advantage in checking work assignments.

The most important thing is to keep the new Christian responding to the leading of the Holy Spirit day by day. This will mean minding God in every detail that he or she understands. Where such obedience is practiced as an inviolable rule of life, Christians, whether new or more mature, should be full of grace, overflowing with the joy of revival.

All along the way, the Christian life is meant to be victorious even as it is constantly expanding in the realization of the glory of Christ. There will be times of great testing, but through it all the obedient pilgrim should be victorious, walking in fellowship with the Son of God whose blood cleanses from all sin. Continuing follow-up consists largely in keeping this truth in focus and interpreting it in life situations as they arise.

Growth by Groups

Raising children is a family affair, so more than individual guidance is needed. There needs to be a warm association within the church. The small-group fellowship is the most natural way to provide this environment. Within this company of believers, a new Christian learns what it means to be a member of the family of God. Already discussed in connection with revival preparation, the small-group principle applies equally in revival follow-up. In fact, the same pattern that produced revival is the way to keep it.

A confirmation or membership training class may be one way to provide this nurture for the first few months.[9] Where the person-to-person concept of follow-up is operating, such a class can give helpful structure to a disciplined course of study. After the course is completed, the group may want to form some kind of continuing fellowship.

Congregational Life

Beyond these small groups, every Christian should feel a part of the larger fellowship of the church. Participation in

the worship services should become a habit. The same is true
of the Sunday school, the missionary society, social functions, retreats—all of these activities help one grow in the
family of God, and each in their own way can contribute to
the continuing spirit of revival.

From time to time the church can have special programs to accentuate spiritual devotion. Some of these services may follow the pattern of the revival meeting. The
church doesn't have to be in a low spiritual ebb to have a
spiritual life crusade. It is much better to have such a series
of services when the congregation already enjoys a high
degree of Christian experience. Where this is the case, the
crusade simply helps to keep the church awake to her
responsibilities even as it offers renewed opportunity for an
evangelistic harvest.

Education with Purpose

All of these means of Christian development should lead to
evangelism. Nurturing the faithful is essential, but as we
have seen, it must always be done within the context of the
church's mission to a lost world. Any time the church
becomes preoccupied with her own interests, she loses the
radiance of the self-giving love of Christ and, unwittingly, in
trying to save her life, she loses it.

No temptation is more beguiling than this. After all, is
there not a legitimate need to protect the gains of the revival?
How then can the revival continue unless its children are
nourished in the faith?

Clearly, a vigorous educational program is indispensable
if the work is to go on. The danger lies in making education

of the saints an end in itself. The zeal for Christian education has a subtle way of pushing evangelism to the periph-
ery, though it does not have to. When it does happen, not
only does the educational program flounder for lack of direction, but the nerve of revival is paralyzed.

The remedy does not lie in minimizing either education
or evangelism. Both are essential. One produces soul-win-
ners, while the other produces soul-winning. The point is
that each must lead to the other. "Education without evangelism makes Pharisees; evangelism without education makes
fanatics."[10]

The Great Commission Lifestyle

Keeping it all together, giving balance and direction to follow-
up, is the mandate of the Great Commission. Christ doesn't
ask us to make converts, though certainly people must be
converted to enter the kingdom of heaven (Matthew 18:3).
The command of our Lord is to "make disciples" (Matthew
28:19)—persons who, having believed the Gospel, now follow Christ in continuing obedience of faith.[11]

Here is the master strategy of Jesus to build His Church
and to raise up a people who will praise Him from the ends
of the earth. For as disciples are made for Christ, they not
only grow in the beauty of His holiness, they also become
involved in the outreach of His ministry. Given proper nurture, disciples invariably become disciplers, and the cycle of
reproduction repeats itself. As new disciples in turn teach
other believers the way of Christ, through the process of multiplication, finally the whole world will have opportunity to
know Him whom the Father has sent (John 17:20-23).

The Great Commission, then, brings the ministry of Christ into the experience of every child of God. Making disciples is a way of life—the way Jesus chose to direct His life while He was among us and now the way we are bidden to follow in His steps.[12]

Leadership the Key

The key again is leadership. People are waiting for someone to show them the way. They are generally open to instruction. God has prepared His harvest. The only limitation is a lack of harvesters—shepherds who will lead the sheep (Matthew 9:36-38).

The entire program of the church, indeed, the whole course of life, revolves around shepherds. In a very real sense, we are today where our leaders have taken us, and our experience is a reflection of their lives. But just as we have followed, so also we have led. "No man is an island unto himself." Whether we live for Christ or self, our witness has its inevitable influence upon those around us, who in turn lead others.

The need is for workers in the harvest who themselves are led by the Spirit of Christ—men and women who follow the Master so consistently that their lives always point the way to Him who is the Great Shepherd of the sheep.

When the church is led by such persons of vision and dedication, regardless of the policy followed, continuing fruitfulness results. But where this kind of personnel is lacking, however excellent the plans and programs may be, the church will flounder in the slough of aimlessness.

Ultimately, the test of revival is the way it reproduces servants of Christ who will pour their lives into others. In the final analysis, this is the genius of every enduring spiritual awakening.

As those who have found spiritual strength go forth to show by their changed lives what God has done *in* them, it will not be long before God will show what He can do *through* them. Here is the reward of revival—the satisfaction of seeing the investment of labor returning multiplied dividends in the lives of matured Christians reproducing their kind in an ever-enlarging sphere of influence unto the ends of the earth and unto the end of time.

Study Assignments 7

Personal Study

1. What is there about young converts that makes follow-up imperative? Ephesians 4:14 (1 Peter 2:2)

2. How did Paul look upon his relationship to new Christians? 1 Thessalonians 2:11 (Galatians 4:19)

3. What was there about most of the early church meetings that provided such a good environment for this family relationship? Acts 2:2, 46; 5:42; 12:12; 16:40 (Romans 16:5; 1 Corinthians 16:19; Colossians 4:15; Philemon 2)

4. What is expected of each person in the family of God according to Ephesians 4:13-15? Sum up your thoughts in a sentence.

5. How does Christ dwelling in you especially attest to spiritual development? Ephesians 3:17-19 (1 Thessalonians 3:12; 1 Corinthians 13)

6. What is a normal expression of maturity in terms of practical service? Hebrews 5:12 (1 Corinthians 3:1-3)

7. Read Paul's farewell message to the elders of the church at Ephesus in Acts 20:17-38. What does he charge these leaders to remember?

Why was he so concerned for this great revival church? Acts 20:29-30

What was the means by which the church was to be built up in the faith according to Acts 20:32?

Yet why do you suppose that Paul gave so much attention to his own example among them for three years? Note Acts 20:17-26, 31, 33-35. In answering this question, think back through the Bible and especially the Gospels.

8. Then if you are to train leaders in the church, what must you do above all else? Philippians 3:17; 4:9 (1 Corinthians 11:1)

9. To put this truth in better focus, paraphrase 2 Timothy 2:2.

10. As you look at your own life, do you see this principle in operation? Are you leading newer Christians in the way of Jesus, and are you teaching them in turn to lead faithful people who will likewise teach others? How? If you are not satisfied, what do you plan to do about it?

Of course, it comes down finally to your own experience of Christ. Do those who look at you see the marks of Jesus? In short, is your life an example of spiritual reality, which is revival?

Group Discussion

With this study drawing to a close, it is only natural that you center your concern upon reproduction. The personal Bible study has lifted out the idea, but you need to get down now to the application of these principles in your church. Perhaps it would be well to let each person tell how he or she was nurtured in the faith during those first years as a Christian. The home doubtless will be the stabilizing factor in most instances, as it should be, but what did the church do to help? From here consider the fruitfulness of your present policy. Now would be a good time to lay some plans for definite implementation of any suggestions for improvement.

NOTES

1. What is most heartbreaking, as things continue to drift, the time comes when indifference gives way to resentment, and the descendants of the revival eventually deny the faith that gave them birth. They may continue to pay lip service to their spiritual heritage and even build impressive memorials to venerate their fathers, but their heart is not in it. Likewise, many of the good "side-effects" of the revival may go on for generations in the life and culture of the people, but even these in time seem to run their course. In fact, many of the institutions such as colleges and seminaries started in revivals eventually change their direction so completely that they become agents of oppression against those who still seek to maintain the original revival spirit.

2. Some good introductions to the subject of follow-up are Waylon B. Moore's volume, *New Testament Follow-up for Pastors and Laymen* (Grand Rapids: Wm. B. Eerdmans, 1972); Charles Riggs, *Learning to Walk with God* (Minneapolis: World Wide Publications, 1986); Gary Kuhne, *The Dynamics of Personal Follow-up* (Grand Rapids: Wm. B. Eerdmans, 1976); Charles Shaver, *Conserve the Converts* (Kansas City: Beacon Hill Press, 1976); Frances M. Cosgrove, *Essentials of the New Life* (Colorado Springs: NavPress, 1978); and Billy Hanks, Jr., *If You Love Me* (Waco: Word, 1985). Above all, read Dawson Trotman's *Born to Reproduce* (Lincoln, Neb.: Back to the Bible, 1957). The founder of The Navigators sums up in this straightforward message the most sensible method of winning and training men to reproduce the Gospel.

3. This is usually called an "adoption" or "sponsor" plan. The way such a committee is set up would depend on the local church structure. The pastor or a leading layperson could be its chairman. Personnel on the committee should be representative of the church, with special attention given to the youth department. It might function as a part of a larger body such as the commission on evangelism or even the church board. Normally it would want to meet at least monthly, though its function should be immediate as the need arises. For a good treatment of the organization and work of such a committee, see Moore, *Follow-up*, 80-106.

4. For example, the seeker might be asked, "Jim, why did you come forward tonight?" The idea is to get the person to state the reason for coming. If one does not know, as sometimes happens, then the counselor may help the person locate the problem by asking probing questions such as, "Jim, did you sense an uncertainty about your salvation?" Until the counselor is certain that the need is met, the seeker is not ready to go (although he may want to be left alone to pray).

Lack of assurance of salvation is a common follow-up problem. It may be caused by one of four things: (1) A misunderstanding of God's promises. Some people have the mistaken idea that assurance of salvation is the privilege of only a few especially pious people. In this case it would be well to ponder 1 John 5:11-13 and, as a follow-up, to read through the whole letter of 1 John, noting each time that the word *know* is used. (2) The seeker may lack confidence because of a faulty understanding of what assurance means. Usually the problem centers in getting assurance mixed up with feelings. In this case the person should be shown that the witness of the Spirit is to the fact of belonging to Christ whether there is an emotional overflow or not (see Romans 8:14-16). (3) It is also possible that the seeker does not understand clearly the conditions for assurance of salvation. In this case attention should be directed to the meaning of repentance, faith, and obedience. (4) If the person still does not have the witness of the Spirit, then it could only be due to failure to respond fully to the will of God.

Every Christian has the right to know that his or her relationship with Christ is a present reality. See my Bible study for new Christians, *Established by the Word of God* (Wilmore, Ky.: Christian Outreach, 1968), or any number of other good follow-up Bible studies.

5. The counselor need not go into a long discussion about the necessity of these Christian practices. The respondent simply needs to be reminded to read the Bible every day, perhaps beginning with the gospel of John, and to pray every day, possibly a minimum of fifteen minutes. (Remember, the person is just a spiritual baby.) Then, of course, he needs to be encouraged to become involved in church life. Usually the new disciple will readily agree to these things. The follow-up worker can enlarge upon these disciplines in subsequent meetings.

6. It would be wise to give the new convert only what can be read within the next day or so. Larger Bible study books should be introduced later when there is more leisure to explain their use. Excellent materials may be obtained from the Billy Graham Evangelistic Association, The Navigators, Campus Crusade for Christ, Inter-Varsity Christian Fellowship, Christian Outreach, International Evangelism Association, and other interdenominational organizations. Many denominational publishing houses also offer materials along this line, and of course a church should use these whenever possible.

7. In making this introduction, give opportunity for the convert to express his or her new commitment. For example, "Bill Smith, I would like you to meet John Doe. I know that he will want to tell you what God has done in his life." This is a natural way to get the new disciple to share a testimony.

8. Most of these contacts can be casual meetings in the normal activity of the day—having a coffee break together at work, coming home together on the bus, going to a ball game, or attending a P.T.A. meeting or church service. The less rigid the visits, the better. However, the informality of these contacts does not minimize the importance of the things discussed. Though it may not be immediately apparent to the new Christian, the fellowship friend has a definite purpose in mind in these calls. Progress in the Christian life is expected, and the counselor is always checking up on how things are going. Progress reports can then be relayed through proper channels to the church officers.

9. The pastor usually is the teacher, though other leaders can handle it. The class normally meets for an hour each week. Basic instruction is given in the doctrine, history, and discipline of the church. Normally all who formally come into the fellowship of the church are expected to take the course. Manuals for use in these classes can be obtained from any denominational publishing house.

10. George E. Sweazey, *Effective Evangelism*, rev. ed. (New York: Harper and Row, 1976), 189.

11. The word *disciple* translates "learner" or "follower" in the sense of an apprentice. As used in the Gospels, the term always implies "a personal attachment that shapes the whole life of the one described." *Theological Dictionary of the New Testament*, ed. Gerhard Kittel, trans. and ed. Geoffrey W. Bromiley, vol. 4 (Grand Rapids: Wm. B. Eerdmans, 1967), 441; cf. Coleman, *The Mind of the Master*, 7-8.

12. There is no want of material on the practical aspects of discipling. In addition to books already cited, including my own *The Master Plan of Evangelism* and *The Master Plan of Discipleship*, check into books published by NavPress, such as Bill Hull, *Jesus Christ Disciple Maker* (1984); Roy Robertson, *The Timothy Principle* (1986); Beth Mainhood, *Reaching Your World* (1986); and Leroy Eims, *The Lost Art of Disciple Making* (1978). Also, from other publishers, Keith Phillips, *The Making of a Disciple* (Old Tappan, N.J.: Fleming Revell, 1981); Carl Wilson, *With Christ in the School of Disciple Building* (Grand Rapids: Zondervan, 1976); and Walter Henrichsen, *Disciples Are Made, Not Born* (Wheaton, Ill.: Victor Books, 1974). A selection of writings in this field are compiled by Billy Hanks, Jr., and William A. Shell in *Discipleship* (Grand Rapids: Zondervan, 1981). One of the best materials on this subject I have seen is the self-study course, complete with eight hours of teaching on audio tapes, entitled *Discipleship: Training Leaders to Make Disciples*, published by the Billy Graham Center Institute of Evangelism at Wheaton (1994).

Eight

The Hope of a Coming World Revival

OUR PRIMARY FOCUS TO THIS POINT HAS BEEN UPON revival in the present context of your own life and church. Yet we cannot separate what God does in your personal experience from His plan to raise up a holy people to praise Him from every tongue and tribe and nation. His Kingdom embraces the whole world, and to that end His Church has been sent to proclaim the Gospel to every creature. What is more, we go forth in the confidence that someday the harvest will be gathered from the ends of the earth. This promise certainly accentuates the possibility of a mighty cosmic revival before the end of the age. Is this hope realistic? If so, it gives us reason to walk on tiptoes.

An Exciting Prophecy

Considering the convulsive struggles of our civilization, any discussion of last things seems relevant today. The growing concern for the world's unreached billions and how the Church will reach them makes the subject even more pertinent.[1]

Scripture does point to some kind of a climactic spiritual conflagration, though the time and extent of its coming can be variously understood. Most of the references to this coming world revival are bound up with other historical situations such as the return of the Jews from captivity and the restoration of their nation. How one understands the Millennium, tribulation, and Rapture must also be taken into account. Obviously, those who see Christ returning to take away His Church before His millennial reign will look at the awakening from a different perspective than those who view it as an aspect of the Millennium. Notwithstanding the differences, nothing in the varying positions necessarily precludes a coming world revival.[2]

Let us admit that the complexity of the biblical prophecies makes any conclusion tentative. Yet, recognizing that we now only see through the glass darkly, it is possible to discern an outline of a future movement of revival that will make anything seen thus far pale by comparison.

A Universal Outpouring of the Holy Spirit

The day is envisioned when the Church in all parts of the world will know the overflow of God's presence. No one will be excluded, as Joel prophesied, "And it shall come to pass afterward, that I will pour out my spirit upon all flesh; and your sons and your daughters shall prophesy, your old men shall dream dreams, your young men shall see visions: And also upon the servants and upon the handmaids in those days will I pour out my spirit" (Joel 2:28-29), a statement clearly indicating that all classes of people from around the world will feel the impact of this spiritual rejuvenation.[3]

Peter associated this promise with the coming of the Holy Spirit at Pentecost (Acts 2:16-17). Yet the universal dimension of the prophecy of Joel was not experienced fully in that the Spirit did not then come upon God's people all over the world. Of course, potentially the first Pentecostal visitation reached to "all flesh," even to them that "are afar off" (Acts 2:39). This was typified by the Spirit-filled disciples' witness to the people present that day from "every nation under heaven" (Acts 2:5).[4] But in actual extent that outpouring was confined to the city. As the Church gradually moved out in the strength of the Holy Spirit, the flame spread to Judea, to Samaria, and finally to many distant places of the civilized world. The message is still going out. But complete fulfillment of the prophecy awaits a glorious day to come.

Certainly a spiritual awakening around the world would be in keeping with the all-embracing love of God (John 3:16). In a dramatic way, it would give notice of the gospel mandate to reach "the uttermost part of the earth" (Acts 1:8; cf. Mark 16:15; John 20:21; Matthew 28:19), fulfilling at last the promise to Abraham that in him all peoples on the earth shall be blessed (Genesis 12:3; 22:18). The worship of God by all the families of the nations, so long foretold, would then be a reality (see Psalms 22:27; 86:9; Isaiah 49:6; Daniel 7:14; Revelation 15:4), and God's name would be great among the Gentiles "from the rising of the sun even unto the going down of the same" (Malachi 1:11).[5]

According to this reasoning, the church age began and will end in a mighty spiritual baptism. What happened at the first Pentecost may be seen as the "early" display of the refreshing rain from heaven, while the closing epic is the "latter rain" (Joel 2:23; Hosea 6:3; Zechariah 10:1; James 5:7). Water or rain, it will be remembered, is often symbolic of the Holy Spirit (John 7:37-39).

Strange Demonstrations of Power

In describing the Spirit's outpouring, Joel foretells "wonders in the heavens and in the earth—blood, fire, and pillars of smoke. The sun shall be turned into darkness, and the moon into blood, before the great and the terrible day of the Lord come" (Joel 2:30-31; cf. Acts 2:19-20). Yet these phenomena are not mentioned as happening in the account of the first Pentecost,[6] so apparently they are yet to occur.

Jesus spoke of days immediately "after the tribulation" in similar terms, adding that "the stars shall fall from heaven, and the powers of the heavens shall be shaken" (Matthew 24:29; cf. Revelation 6:12-13). It seems that God will summon the forces of nature to bear witness to what is happening on the earth.

Adding to the spectacle, some persons will have the power to perform wondrous deeds, such as turning water to blood (Revelation 11:6; cf. Galatians 3:5). Naturally, Satan will do what he can to counterfeit what he knows is real. We are warned of "false Christs" and "false prophets" of this time who will show "great signs and wonders" to deceive the elect (Matthew 24:24; cf. Exodus 7:10-12; Matthew 7:15-20; 2 Thessalonians 2:9-10). The sensory appeal is always fraught with danger, which is all the more reason why we are exhorted to try the spirits. If they are not Christ-exalting, then they are not of God (1 John 4:1-3).

Unprecedented Trouble

Those fearful conditions of the last days described in Matthew 24 and intermittently in Revelation 6 to 17 also seem to characterize this period. And things will get worse as the end approaches (cf. 2 Timothy 3:12; 2 Thessalonians 2:1-3).

Famines, pestilence, and earthquakes of staggering proportions will occur. Wars and intrigue will fill the earth. Hate will bind the hearts of men. No one will feel secure. As moral integrity breaks down, apostasy in the Church will increase. Those who do not conform to the spirit of the age will be hard pressed, and many will be martyred. Clearly, the cost of discipleship will be high.[7]

Yet amid this terrible adversity, Scripture indicates that revival will sweep across the earth. When God's "judgments are in the earth, the inhabitants of the world will learn righteousness" (Isaiah 26:9). Dreadful calamities will mingle with awesome displays of salvation—the terrors will actually create an environment for earnest heart-searching. Not everyone will turn to God, of course. Some persons will remain unrepentant and become even more brazen in their sin. But the world will be made to confront as never before the Cross of Jesus Christ.

How it will all end is not clear. Possibly the revival will close, and there will be "a falling away" before the Lord returns (2 Thessalonians 2:3).[8] Some Bible students believe that the worst tribulation will come after the Church is caught up. Others think that Christians will be taken out of the world midway through this dreadful period.

However viewed, Scripture gives us no reason to think that the last great revival will avert the coming catastrophe. The point of no return will have already been passed.

Judgment is certain. Revival may delay, but it will not prevent the final day of reckoning.

Cleansing of the Church

Through the purging of revival, God's people will be brought to the true beauty of holiness. Our Lord expects to present His bride unto Himself "a radiant church, without stain or wrinkle or any other blemish, but holy and blameless" (Ephesians 5:27 NIV; cf. 1 John 3:2-3; 2 Corinthians 7; 1 Peter 1:13-16; 3:4). The trials of the last days will serve as fires to refine the gold of Christian character. Out of them the bride of Christ, "arrayed in fine linen, clean and white," will emerge ready for the marriage supper of the Lamb (Revelation 19:7-9; cf. Daniel 12:10). To this end, the "latter rain" of the Spirit is intended to bring "the precious fruit" of the Church to maturity in preparation for the Lord's return (James 5:7; cf. Song of Solomon 2).

The Church should not fear affliction though it cause anguish and even death. Suffering may be necessary to convince us that we do not live by bread alone. When received as an expression of God's trust, our suffering can be a means of helping us comprehend more of the love of Christ, who "suffered for us, leaving us an example, that ye should follow his steps" (1 Peter 2:21; cf. Heb. 2:10; 5:8). Without hardship, probably few of us would learn much about the deeper life of grace.

A purified Church will be able to receive unhindered the power of the outpoured Spirit and thereby more boldly enter into the mission of Christ. It is also reasonable to believe that this greater concurrence with God's program will multiply the manifestation of ministry gifts in the body (Ephesians 3:7-15; cf. Romans 12:6-8; 1 Corinthians 12:4-11; 1 Peter

4:10-11). This would further call attention to the momentous awakening on earth.

Tremendous Ingathering of Souls

The coming world revival will naturally result in multitudes calling upon the name of the Lord for salvation (Joel 2:32; Acts 2:21; cf. Romans 10:13). And the same revival will also prepare workers for that great harvest of souls. People full of the Holy Spirit are committed to God's work. They want to be where laborers are needed most, and there is no more pressing need than bringing the Gospel to hell-bound men and women.

Significantly, Jesus said that the fulfillment of His preaching mission would precede His return: "This gospel of the Kingdom will be preached in the whole world as a testimony to all nations, and then the end will come" (Matthew 24:14 NIV; cf. Luke 12:36-37; 14:15-23). Doubtless the passion to get out the message while there is yet time will increase with the revival, even as the witnesses multiply. That the Gospel will eventually penetrate "every nation, tribe, people and language" is clear from the description of the innumerable multitude of the white-robed saints gathered around the throne of God in heaven (Revelation 7:9 NIV; cf. 5:9). The Great Commission will finally be fulfilled.

Many believe that Jews will be among the lost who turn to Christ at that time. At least some prophecies speak of their general repentance and acceptance of the Messiah (see Ezekiel 20:43-44; Jeremiah 31:34; Romans 11:24) and of God's pardon and blessing (see Jeremiah 31:27-34; 32:37–33:26; Ezekiel 16:60-63; 37:1-28; Hosea 6:1-2; Amos 9:11-15; Revelation 7:1-17). The world revival seems a logical time for this to happen. Pretribulationists might put the Jewish awakening after the rapture of the Church, making a great deal of Romans 11:25-26, which speaks of Israel's being saved when the fulness of the Gentiles is come.[9] This passage, however, could serve equally well to support the idea of revival before Christ comes again.

Whatever position one might hold, without a doubt the greatest day of evangelism is before us. The harvesting may be short in duration and may require enormous sacrifice, but it will be the most far-reaching acceptance of the Gospel this world has ever seen.

Preparing for Christ's Return

The massive turning to Christ by people from the four corners of the earth will prepare the way for the coming of the King. Our Lord's return may be waiting now on this spiritual revolution. "Behold, the husbandman waiteth for the precious fruit of the earth, and hath long patience for it, until he receive the early and latter rain. Be ye also patient; establish your hearts: for the coming of the Lord draweth nigh" (James 5:7-8).

The fact that our Lord has not already returned to establish His kingdom is evidence of His desire to see the Church perfected and the Gospel presented to every person for whom He died. God is "longsuffering to us-ward, not willing that any should perish, but that all should come to repentance" (2 Peter 3:9). But we dare not presume upon His patience. None of us can be so sure of our understanding of prophecy as to preclude His return at any moment. Every day we should be ready to meet the Lord, the more so as we see the night approaching![10]

Anticipation of our Lord's return is a summons to

action. We must cast off anything that blocks the flow of the Holy Spirit and commit ourselves to being about the Father's business. World evangelization now is the responsibility around which our lives should be centered. Whatever our gifts, we are all needed in the witness of the Gospel.

Uniting in Prayer

As we anticipate the coming world revival, prayer is our greatest resource. The prophet reminds us, "Ask ye of the Lord rain in the time of the latter rain" (Zechariah 10:1). "When the tongue faileth for thirst," God says, "I will open rivers in high places, and fountains in the midst of the valleys" (Isaiah 41:18; cf. 44:3). Surely it is time to "seek the Lord, till he come and rain righteousness" upon us (Hosea 10:12; cf. Joel 2:17; Acts 1:14). There is no other way to bring life to the Church and hope to the barren fields of the world.

As the first Great Awakening swept America in 1748, Jonathan Edwards, responding to a proposal from church leaders in Scotland, published *A Humble Attempt to Promote Explicit Agreement and Visible Union of God's People in Extraordinary Prayer, for the Revival of Religion and the Advancement of Christ's Kingdom on Earth, Pursuant to Scripture Promises and Prophecies Concerning the Last Time.* It was an appeal for the Church to unite in earnest intercession for world revival based on the text of Zechariah 8:20-21:

> It shall yet come to pass, that there shall come people, and the inhabitants of many cities: And the inhabitants of one city shall go to another, saying, Let us go speedily to pray before the Lord, and to seek the Lord of hosts: I will go

also. Yea, many people and strong nations shall come to
seek the Lord of hosts. . . .

About this passage Edwards said:

From the representation mode in this prophecy, it appears
. . . that it will be fulfilled something after this manner; first,
that there shall be given much of a spirit of prayer to God's
people in many places, disposing them to come into an
express agreement, unitedly to pray to God in an extraordinary manner, that he would appear for the help of his
church, and in mercy to mankind, and to pour out his
Spirit, revive his work, and advance his spiritual kingdom
in the world as he has promised; and that this disposition
to such prayer, and union in it, will spread more and more,
and increase in greater degrees; with which at length will
gradually be introduced a revival of religion, and a disposition to greater eagerness in the worship and service of God,
amongst his professing people; that this being observed,
will be the means of awakening others, making them sensible of the wants of their souls, and exciting in them a great
concern for their spiritual and everlasting good, and putting
them upon earnest crying to God for spiritual mercies, and
disposing them to join with God's people . . . and that in
this manner religion shall be propagated, until the awakening reaches these that are in the highest stations, and until
whole nations be awakened, and there be at length an acces-
sion of many of the chief nations of the world to the church
of God. . . . And thus that shall be fulfilled: "O thou that
hearest prayer, unto thee shall all flesh come" (Psalm 65:2).[11]

Edwards's plea for God's people to come together in fervent and constant prayer for revival still speaks with urgency.
Not only does it call us to our most essential ministry of

intercession, but it also reminds us of the way God has ordained to quicken His Church and to disseminate her witness until finally the nations of the earth shall come and worship before the Lord.

Living in Expectancy

Billy Graham in his last message at the Lausanne Congress in 1974 expressed succinctly both the realism and the hope we have in awaiting "the climactic movement and the total fulfillment of what was done on the Cross." Then, reflecting upon the future, he added:

> I believe there are two strains in prophetic Scripture. One leads us to understand that as we approach the latter days and the Second Coming of Christ, things will become worse and worse. Joel speaks of "multitudes, multitudes in the valley of decision!" The day of the Lord is near in the valley of decision. He is speaking of judgment.
>
> But I believe as we approach the latter days and the coming of the Lord, it could be a time also of great revival. We cannot forget the possibility and the promise of revival, the refreshing of the latter days of the outpouring of the Spirit promised in Joel 2:28 and repeated in Acts 2:17. That will happen right up to the advent of the Lord Jesus Christ.
>
> Evil will grow worse, but God will be mightily at work at the same time. I am praying that we will see in the next months and years the "latter rains," a rain of blessings, showers falling from heaven upon all the continents before the coming of the Lord.[12]

All of us should join in this prayer even as we look expectantly to what lies ahead. Something great is on the horizon.

You can almost feel it in the air. Though forces of evil are becoming more sinister and aggressive, there is a corresponding cry for spiritual awakening. Across the world never has there been more yearning by more people for spiritual reality, nor has the Church ever had the means it now has to take the glad tidings of salvation to the lost, unreached peoples of the earth. What a day to be alive!

Certainly this is not a time for despair. The King's coming is certain. And in preparation for His return we may be the generation that will see the greatest revival since the beginning of time.

Study Assignments 8

Personal Study

1. Reflect upon the context of Joel's prophecy with its dual reference to his own day and to the future. Note the calamities that have come upon the land, reminding the people of their sin, and the call to repent (Joel 1:1–2:17). How does God promise to respond to their cries (Joel 2:18–3:21)?

Relate the "day of the Lord" both to the immediate situation and to the ultimate hope.

2. How was Joel's prophecy fulfilled at Pentecost (Acts 2:1-42)? In what way is the promise still being fulfilled? At what time will it be totally fulfilled?

3. In what way is "the latter rain" associated with the outpouring of the Spirit and the completion of the harvest (James 5:7; cf. Joel 2:23)? Why is it associated with patience while waiting for the coming of the Lord?

4. Read the signs surrounding the return of Christ in Matthew 24:1-51. Why would the terrible events to transpire on earth contribute to the preaching of the Gospel around the world (Matthew 24:14)?

5. As you understand revival, why would it bring the Church finally to complete the Great Commission of Christ?

In terms of your present experience, how is the Spirit's fulness inseparable from making disciples?

6. What signs of spiritual awakening do you see in the world today?

7. Looking to the day of Christ's glorious return, how do you see your church preparing for His coming? What about you? Are you living in a state of readiness?

Group Discussion

Since this is your final meeting, project your thinking to the future. Let the members of the group share their answers to the questions in the study. Doubtless there will be differences of opinion, but the possibility of a great world revival should give the discussion an upbeat note. In light of your expectations, plan to keep moving on to higher ground.

You may want to meet again as a group to continue your fellowship around the Word of God. It might even be that your group could become a home for others seeking the reality of Christ. Decide together what course you should follow in the future.

NOTES

1. The substance of this chapter first appeared in *Christianity Today*, July 16, 1971, and is used by permission. A reprint of the article is in *Perspectives in the World Christian Movement*, a reader edited by Ralph D. Winter and Steven C. Hawthorne (Pasadena: William Carey Library, 1981), 355-58.

2. Strangely the idea of a last great world revival is given little specific mention in biblical theology, although it is often implied. Martin Bucer, the mentor of John Calvin, seems to be one of the first advocates, in his development of

Augustinian amillennialism, by projecting a widespread conversion of Jews following the reformation of the Church. With some modifications, this view became common among Puritans such as John Owen and William Perkins and Pietists such as Jakob Spener and J. A. Bengel. For more information, see Peter Toon, *Puritans, the Millennium and the Future of Israel: Puritan Eschatology, 1600 to 1660* (Cambridge: James Clarke & Co., 1970) and Ian Murray, *The Puritan Hope* (London: Banner of Truth Trust, 1971). In the seventeenth century some theologians moved to a premillennial position, adopting the presuppositions characteristic of the early church fathers. Others took a more postmillennial turn, a view that largely dominated the thought of eighteenth- and early nineteenth-century American revival teachers such as Philip Doddridge, Jonathan Edwards, and later Charles G. Finney.

Yet as Richard F. Lovelace points out, in this spectrum of millennial opinion there was unanimity in the teaching of a great world awakening, "since even the premillennialists believed that the outpouring of the Spirit and the conversion of large numbers of Jews and Gentiles would precede the millennium" (*Dynamics of Spiritual Life*, 408). This thinking among revival-minded premillennialists, positive amillennialists, and postmillennialists continued into the middle of the nineteenth century. As a more liberal social agenda absorbed the thrust for renewal, most evangelicals, following Moody, adopted some form of premillennialism, a trend that has continued into the twentieth century.

3. The inclusion of the young, the women, and the servants—persons at that time usually least expected to receive divine favor—underscores the totality of the blessing. That priests, prophets, and kings are mentioned—people usually most associated with leadership—makes the point even more impressive.

4. The fifteen nations mentioned in verses 9-11, while not inclusive of every group in the world, could be said to represent "people from all over the known world" (I. Howard Marshall, *The Acts of the Apostles* [Grand Rapids: Wm. B. Eerdmans, 1980], 71; cf. Richard B. Rockham, *The Acts of the Apostles* [Grand Rapids: Baker Book House, 1964], 22).

5. It is interesting to note that the modern missionary movement was rooted in the optimism inspired by such exponents of world revival as Jonathan Edwards, reflected in his edition of David Brainerd's *Diary*, and Isaac Watts, as seen in his hymn "Jesus Shall Reign." It was this longing for the universal reign of Christ that burned in the heart of missionaries like William Carey, Henry Martyn, and Charles Simeon, causing them to recite again and again Habakkuk's prophecy: "For the earth shall be filled with the knowledge of the glory of the Lord, as the waters cover the sea" (Habakkuk 2:14). In addition to Lovelace, *Dynamics*, 409-10, see J. A. de Jong, *As the Waters Cover the Sea: Millennial Expectations in the Rise of Anglo-American Missions, 1640-1810* (Kampen: Kok, 1970).

6. I. Howard Marshall observes that if we do not accept that the reference is to the cosmic signs that accompanied the Crucifixion (Luke 23:44-45), then it looks "forward to the signs which shall herald the end of the world; these are still future, and they belong to the 'end' of the last days, rather than to their 'beginning,' which is just taking place." (*The Acts of the Apostles*, 74).

7. Significantly, in recent years the number of Christians tortured or executed for their faith has been rising. According to research consultant David Barrett, approximately 335,000 persons now are martyred each year, and it is estimated that the annual average will climb to 500,000 by the year 2000. "As a 'sign from God'," he says, "this appalling statistic warns us about the escalating conflict between church and state, and hence our future prospects in global missions" (David Barrett, "Annual Statistical Table—Global Missions: 1987," *International Bulletin of Missionary Research* 2, no. 1, [January 1987], 24; cf. context in *Christianity Today* 32, no. 1, [January 15, 1988], 27).

8. During this awful time some are said to "have repented not" (Revelation 9:20-21; 16:9). The fact that their refusal to repent is called to our attention indicates that the opportunity was there to repent. However, the absence of even these negative references toward the close of the period as Armageddon approaches might indicate opportunity for repentance is finally withdrawn by God.

9. Those who believe that the tribulation will follow the rapture of the Church may still allow for a Gentile revival before the Lord's return, thus anticipating two distinct revivals in the end time.

10. It is this expectancy of the Lord's personal, visible, historical return in the clouds of glory that distinguishes evangelical faith—not any one particular view of the Millennium or a revival in the end time. Let us always keep this truth in focus—Jesus is coming again—and where this "blessed hope" of the Church is unequivocally affirmed, we will agree to disagree on the way events related to His second coming are interpreted.

11. Jonathan Edwards, *A Humble Attempt . . .* , *The Works of President Edwards*, vol. 3 (New York: Leavitt, Trow and Co., 1818), 432-33. The full discourse, encompassing pages 423-508, lifts up the promise of world revival and the need to pray unitedly for it more than any other writing in the English language. The appeal for concerts of prayer also comes out in George Whitefield's ministry during this same period and, indeed, continued in revival efforts through the nineteenth century. In recent years it has been picked up again by such international voices as the Lausanne Committee for World Evangelization and A.D. 2000. For a contemporary exposition of the movement and practical direction in how you can become involved, see Robert Bakke, *The Concert of Prayer: Back to the Future*, op. cit. and David Bryant's *With Concerts of Prayer* (Ventura, Cal.: Regal Books, 1984) or his more recent *Operation: Prayer* (Madison, Wis.: Inter-Varsity Christian Fellowship, 1987). Historical background is given by J. Edwin Orr in *The Eager Feet: Evangelical Awakenings, 1790-1830* (Chicago: Moody Press, 1975).

12. Billy Graham, "The King Is Coming," in *Let the Earth Hear His Voice*, Official Reference Volume for the International Congress on World Evangelization, Lausanne, Switzerland, ed. J. D. Douglas (Minneapolis: World Wide Publications, 1975), 1466.

Scripture Index

General Index